מסורה

ArtScroll Mesorah Series®

D1319292

Rabbi Nosson Scherman / Rabbi Meir Zlotowitz

General Editors

YESHIVATH
BETH MOSHE

ישיבת
בית משה

930 Hickory Street
Scranton, Pa 18505
(717) 346-1747

Yeshiva Beth Moshe of Scranton — during its more than twenty-five years — has consistently made the dissemination of vital Jewish literature an integral part of its agenda. It is with pride that we participate in this present volume dealing with G-d's beautiful gift to His people — the holy Shabbos.

Just as Shabbos has been one of the pillars of the Jewish nation, so, too, Torah learning has been the backbone of our people. At Beth Moshe, our Kollel, Beis Medrash and Mesivta — approaching an enrollment of nearly two hundred young men — have added a new dimension to Torah scholarship in America.

It is our fervent prayer that in the merit of Shabbos and Torah, that we live to see the coming of Moshiach במהרה בימינו.

אליהו בן ר׳ יעקב צבי

נפטר ט׳ סיון תשכ״ה
June 9, 1965

יוטא בת ר׳ יעקב מרדכי

נפטרה כ״ה אייר תשכ״ה
May 27, 1965

Dedicated to the memory
of our dear departed parents

Elias and Ita Fink

Who taught with love, deed and action
that you could experience
the sanctity and joy of Shabbos,
in any place and in any culture.

Mr. and Mrs. David Fink
and Family
Mt. Cobb. Pennsylvania

לזכר נשמת

In loving memory of
our parents and grandparents

חוה בת יצחק הלל   משה בן צבי
נפ׳ ז׳ ניסן תשל״ד   נפ׳ ו׳ אייר תשמ״א

Moshe and Eva Schwartz
Washington Heights and Israel

חנה בת ארי׳ צבי   אברהם בן משה
נפ׳ ו׳ שבט תשמ״ז   נפ׳ ח׳ תשרי תשל״ח

Abraham and Hannah Kornfeld
Berlin and Wilkes Barre, PA.

Who instilled in us
the true meaning of the saying,
"More than the Jew has kept the Shabbos,
the Shabbos has kept the Jew".

Alvin and Lilly Schwartz
and children
Renee and David
Kingston, Pennsylvania

מצא אשה מצא טוב ויפק רצון מה'

Dedicated to the memory of
Our wife, mother, grandmother and great-grandmother

האשה באשה בת ר' יעקב
Bessie (Hagler) Feller
נפ' ט"ז אלול תשמ"ח

To these tempest tossed shores she came
to fulfill the American dream.
Following in her father's footsteps
she would not compromise her observance of Shabbos.
Back to Europe she went
to fulfill her father's request.
She returned with her mate
to build a home upon the proud tradition of her forefather.
She was a true helpmate to her husband
in his endeavors to bring Yiddishkeit to Coney Island.
She left us with an enduring legacy
of self-sacrifice, love and devotion.

תהי' זכרה ברוך

William Feller

Jerry and Nechama Feller
and Family

Yisroel and Reyna Hisiger
and Family

Published by

Mesorah Publications, ltd

shabbos

**THE SABBATH — ITS ESSENCE AND SIGNIFI-
CANCE** / A PRESENTATION ANTHOLOGIZED
FROM TALMUDIC AND TRADITIONAL SOURCES.

by
Rabbi Shimon Finkelman

Overview by
Rabbi Nosson Scherman

FIRST EDITION
First Impression . . . August, 1990

ARTSCROLL MESORAH SERIES®
SHABBOS / THE SABBATH
© Copyright 1990, by MESORAH PUBLICATIONS, Ltd.
4401 Second Avenue / Brooklyn, N.Y. 11232 / (718) 921-9000

ISBN:
0-89906-603-8 (hard cover)
0-89906-604-6 (paperback)

Typography by Compuscribe at ArtScroll Studios, Ltd.

Printed in the United States of America by Noble Book Press
Bound by Sefercraft, Quality Bookbinders, Ltd. Brooklyn, N.Y.

An Overview —
The Sabbath

I. Man and the Sabbath

The Bridge

Of all of the cogs in creation, only man can be an intelligent beast or a flesh-and-blood angel.

The climax of the *physical* creation was man, the animal being whose primary significance is his spiritual nature. Of all of the cogs in creation, only man is balanced between the material and the spiritual: he can be an intelligent beast or a flesh-and-blood angel. He is the bridge between heaven and earth, always living with the challenge of choosing which part of his nature — body or soul — will dominate. The Sages declare that man was created just before the beginning of the holy Sabbath so that he should enter a period of holiness almost as soon as he came into being.

The Sabbath — how are we to understand it? Is it nothing more than a day of inactivity, a neuter?

The Sabbath — how are we to understand it? Is it nothing more than a day of inactivity, a neuter? Or is it a vital, active day, a day of intense striving?

Indeed, the Sabbath of God, the day He intended Adam to experience almost as soon as he opened his eyes to the paradise of Eden, was a day saturated with purpose. The Torah tells us that God sanctified the Sabbath כִּי בוֹ שָׁבַת מִכָּל מְלַאכְתּוֹ, *because on it He rested from all His work* (*Exodus* 2:3), but the purpose of His rest was לַעֲשׂוֹת, *to make, to accomplish, to do.* He rested on the Sabbath, yet simultaneously He accomplished. Though He rested from *physical* creation, He accomplished new wonders by creating the spiritual universe that comes into being every Sabbath. The world of the Sabbath is far above the world of the six days it supplants, yet the two are not separate from one another.

The Sabbath is far above the six days it supplants, yet the two are not separate from one another.

The Sabbath is
the soul of time.
It infuses holiness
into every aspect
of creation.

The Sabbath is the soul of time. It infuses holiness into
every aspect of creation: וַיְקַדֵּשׁ אֹתוֹ, and He sanctified it
(ibid.). God sanctified the Sabbath by making it the
repository of so much of Creation's holiness and by
making its content the essence of the universe.

It was this concept that the Sages suggested with a
parable about God's motive in creating the day. A king
ordered that a signet ring be fashioned for him. His
artisans presented him with a precious band inlaid with
sparkling gems. It was a thing of beauty — but the *seal*
was lacking. Whatever value the ring might have, it
could not be used as a signet unless it contained the seal
which alone would give it the utility its owner required.
So, too, the universe. It might be a naturalist's paradise,
a scientist's challenge, a tycoon's gold mine — *but the*
King wanted it to be His signet ring. He wanted
Creation to meld all its accouterments into a combined
vehicle for declaring His glory. The newly born
universe was lacking the seal of the King. So He gave it
the Sabbath, the day that proclaims, 'The world has a
Creator and a purpose.' By means of the Sabbath, God's
seal was embedded in Creation and His intention was
fulfilled.

The newly born
universe was
lacking the seal
of the King.
So He gave it
the Sabbath.

In this light we can understand the teaching of the
Sages that God had desired to create man on the
Sabbath, instead of on the sixth day. God is not a
human builder who improvises. His intention and His
performance never contradict one another. If they
appear to be at cross-purposes, it is only because each
represents a different facade of the same unit. God
intended to create man on the Sabbath because his soul
belongs with the holiness of the day. He *created* him on
the sixth day because he is a physical creature whose
body belongs with the animal, vegetable, and mineral
creatures of earth. Man was actually created late on the
sixth day, soon to enter the seventh day; he was a bridge
between the secular six and the sacred seventh because
the purpose of his existence is to bridge the two. God's
intention and His deed complemented one another: one
expresses man's mission, the other refers to the conditions of his existence.

Man was a bridge
between the
secular six and
the sacred seventh
because the
purpose of his
existence is to
bridge the two.

Of all the creatures in the universe, man alone is

capable of creating holiness. Matter and animal life can become sacred, but only if man hallows them. True, the Sabbath is God's seal, but only man can impress its image upon the universe (*Sfas Emes*).

II. Wisdom — The Key to Creation*

Units of Ten

The creation of man as the transition between the six days of labor and the day of rest was crucial to the fulfillment of the Sabbath and the entire universe. Many commentaries (prominently among them is *Chiddushei HaRim*) have noted the close connection between the Ten Utterances with which the universe was created (*Avos* 5:1) and the Ten Commandments given to Israel at Sinai. The number 'ten' is no coincidence. The commandments were — and are — the spiritual purpose for which the world was brought into being. The Ten Utterances created a body; the Ten Commandments infused it with a soul.

The Ten Utterances created a body; the Ten Commandments infused it with a soul.

When the Torah is described as the purpose of creation, it is called a בְּרִית, *covenant:* אִם לֹא בְרִיתִי יוֹמָם וָלַיְלָה חֻקּוֹת שָׁמַיִם וָאָרֶץ לֹא שָׂמְתִּי, *Were it not for My covenant day and night, I would not have established the laws of heaven and earth* (Jeremiah 33:25).

In the familiar interpretation of the Sages, God declares that heaven and earth were created only because Israel was to accept the Torah and study it day and night. Were there to be no acceptance of the Law, or were it ח״ו to be neglected, all existence as we know would cease to be.

A בְּרִית, covenant, represents the understanding that defines and governs the relationship between parties.

A בְּרִית, *covenant*, represents the understanding that defines and governs the relationship between parties. In international law, for example, a treaty supersedes all local laws. The most insignificant ordinance in the tiniest hamlet becomes null and void if its effect tends to violate the provisions of a treaty. Similarly, the very existence of heaven and earth is based on the covenant of God's Torah. Heaven and earth 'live' because within

---

* This section of the Overview is based on *Pachad Yitzchak Kuntres HaShabbos* by *Harav Yitzchok Hutner*.

them is the 'soul' of Torah; the Ten Commandments giving meaning to the Ten Utterances.

Sanctity was injected into the universe as soon as the six days of creation were completed.

To accomplish this purpose, sanctity was injected into the universe as soon as the six days of creation were completed. Only after וַיְכֻלּוּ הַשָּׁמַיִם וְהָאָרֶץ וְכָל צְבָאָם, *Thus the heaven and earth were finished and all their array* (Genesis 2:1), do we find mention of sanctity: וַיְבָרֶךְ אֱלֹהִים אֶת יוֹם הַשְּׁבִיעִי וַיְקַדֵּשׁ אֹתוֹ, *God blessed the seventh day and hallowed it* (ibid. 2:3). As the Midrash teaches (*Bereishis Rabbah* 10:2), the word וַיְכֻלּוּ, *[they] were finished*, is related to כְּלִי, *a vessel, a tool,* i.e., heaven and earth became the *vessels* within which God's will would be contained and the *tools* with which it was to be accomplished. The Sabbath was the "seal" that was embedded on the ring; the world was ready for its purpose.

Assigning Priorities

The status of a vessel or tool is dependent upon the use to which it is put. Identical leather pouches can be used to carry gold coins or children's marbles. If the former, the pouch is a wallet; if the latter, it is a toy. The laws of the Sabbath employ this concept. One of the forbidden labors is *carrying from domain to domain.* Such carrying constitutes a punishable offense, however, only if an item of significance is moved. The Talmud gives examples of such measurements: if the amount transported is too small to be considered of reasonable value, the carrier is not considered to have violated the Scriptural prohibition (see *Shabbos* ch. 8.).

If it is used as a container, its status in terms of the Sabbath laws depends on the contents.

In the case of a vessel, if it is used as a container, its status in terms of the Sabbath laws depends on the contents. For example, if one transports an empty silver cup from his apartment to the street, he is in violation because the object of his interest is the cup itself. If, however, there is wine in the cup, then his motive is to move the wine from one place to another; its utility in *that particular act* is purely as a vessel by means of which the wine can be carried, even if the cup is worth more than its contents.

But the cup *itself* was still transported! Why should the presence of an insignificant ounce or two of wine nullify the considerable value of a silver cup? The answer is that Sabbath labor is Scripturally forbidden only if it is מְלָאכֶת מַחְשֶׁבֶת, a labor done with intention and forethought. As long as the intended accomplishment involved the contents, the container is considered only an accessory. The reality is defined by the motive.

The reality is defined by the motive.

This principle of עִיקָר וְטָפֵל, *priority and accessory*, should not be seen as only a detail among the many and complex laws of the Sabbath. Rather it is fundamental to understanding the essence of the day and its role as the climactic element in Creation. The Heavenly design was that the making of priority judgments be basic in the attainment of His goal. Given that the Torah, as represented by the Ten Commandments, is the *covenant* of creation, what is more essential to man's mission than to define priorities and responsibilities?

The Heavenly design was that the making of priority judgments be basic in the attainment of His goal.

What does God want of me? Will I be performing a *mitzvah* by putting this pot on the stove in honor of the Sabbath, or will it be a transgression because the Sabbath has already begun? Will this occupation enable me to perform God's will more easily because of its financial rewards, or will the resultant temptations lead me astray? Indeed, the very goal of placing the tenfold stages of Creation in the service of the Ten Commandments requires the unending exercise of intelligent judgment.

The very goal of placing the tenfold stages of Creation in the service of the Ten Commandments requires the unending exercise of intelligent judgment.

The Torah's description of the Sabbath as God's day of rest provides an insight into the function of the day:

וַיֹּאמֶר ה' אֶל מֹשֶׁה לֵּאמֹר. וְאַתָּה דַּבֵּר אֶל בְּנֵי יִשְׂרָאֵל לֵאמֹר אַךְ אֶת שַׁבְּתֹתַי תִּשְׁמֹרוּ כִּי אוֹת הִוא בֵּינִי וּבֵינֵיכֶם לְדֹרֹתֵיכֶם לָדַעַת כִּי אֲנִי ה' מְקַדִּשְׁכֶם.

HASHEM said to Moses as follows: You shall speak to the Children of Israel saying, But My Sabbaths you are to observe; for it is a sign between Me and you for your generations, to know that I am HASHEM Who sanctifies you (Exodus 31:12-13).

To Know Thus the Torah makes it clear that Israel is exhorted to observe the Sabbath לָדַעַת, *to know*. The Sabbath is a vehicle of the most essential knowledge of all: the knowledge that God is the source of holiness. Knowledge and the Sabbath are inseparable. Even the definition of forbidden labor is dependent on intention and priority, on מְלֶאכֶת מַחְשֶׁבֶת, the forethought and motive of the doer, the *priority and accessory* status of the components within an act. All depends on the active mind. Such is the law of the Sabbath, and such is the fulfillment of creation: the exercise of intelligent judgment is basic. This knowledge and the Sabbath are inseparable.

All depends on the active mind. Such is the law of the Sabbath, and such is the fulfillment of creation.

The Sabbath Creation

Until the arrival of the first Sabbath, the Ten Utterances of creation had been the controlling factors of the universe. More and more physical creatures and material phenomena were coming into existence. With the beginning of the Sabbath, a new factor was introduced: holiness. The newly completed universe was meant to become subservient to this newly introduced component of creation, to be transformed into a vessel containing sanctity. If holiness was preeminent, then the earth would become its accessory. Conversely, if material riches were paramount, then holiness would be insignificant and the 'vessel' would become paramount. God's wish was that the creation of six days be assigned its proper role as a vessel serving something greater than itself.

If holiness was preeminent, then the earth would become its accessory.

Only one being could facilitate that designation — man. Only man had intelligence as opposed to instinct. Animals would react to conditions. They could sense danger and find water. They could mate with their kind and avoid others. Birds could cross continents and oceans with the change of seasons. But only man could consciously decide that money was an instrument and charity its function, that food was means and spiritual life its end, that earth was a vessel whose value was measured by the holiness that filled it.

Only man could consciously decide that money was an instrument and charity its function.

All of creation is renewed constantly — else it could not exist — but the particular renewal of the Sabbath involves recognition and perception. The condition for *Sabbath's* renewal — man — was created before the Sabbath began. The last utterance of creation was נַעֲשֶׂה אָדָם, *let us make man* (Genesis 1:26). All six days with their pyramiding acts of creation had been building up to the climactic moment when man came into being. He alone could recognize the holiness of the Sabbath and make the intelligent choice that would transform the Ten Utterances of creation into the vessels containing *Only he could* the Ten Commandments. Only he could carry out the *carry out the* covenant of heaven and earth.

covenant of
heaven and earth. Based on the above, *Pachad Yitzchok* explains a teaching of the *Vilna Gaon*. The *Gaon* writes that God constantly renews His act of creation, but that the renewal needed on the Sabbath was prepared beforehand; on the Sabbath itself, God rested, because the essence of His renewal had already been provided. True. Renewal is a function of man, who was created before the Sabbath began.

Sabbath It is instructive that the commandment of the Sabbath *and* precedes that of the festivals throughout the Torah: *Festival* *Exodus 23:12-19, Leviticus 23, Numbers 28.* For that reason, the Sabbath is described in *Kiddush* — the blessing which introduces and defines the day — as תְּחִלָּה לְמִקְרָאֵי קֹדֶשׁ, *the prologue to the holy convocations* (see *comm.* to *Kiddush*).

The precedence given the Sabbath is a reflection of its nature with relation to the festivals. One difference between the two is familiar: The Sabbath, because it was ordained by God, is permanent. Every seventh day is a Sabbath whether or not it is observed. It is designated by God and, as such, is not subject to the actions of people. But the festivals are dependent on the Jewish calendar. Passover, for example, is the fifteenth day of the month of Nissan; if, theoretically, the *Beis Din* were not to proclaim the New Moon, there would be no Nissan and no Passover. [Similarly, certain laws which are dependent on יוֹבֵל, the *Jubilee Year*, cannot be observed in the absence of a Sanhedrin to proclaim the Jubilee Year.]

Thus, the very institution of the festivals is evidence *He can consecrate* of the spiritual power of man: he can consecrate months *months and* *festivals; with* and festivals; with him, there are *holy* days, without *him, there are holy* him there are only days. How does man acquire this *days, without him* *there are only* cosmic power? From the Sabbath! It is the *prologue to* *days.* *the holy convocations.* Because man has the wisdom to differentiate between form and content, because he was given the ability to bring about the renewal of creation on the Sabbath day that demands recognition of the spiritual nature of creation, because he could become the bridge bringing holiness from heaven to earth, he was

He was enabled not only to recognize holiness, but to proclaim it.

given yet another privilege. He was enabled not only to *recognize* holiness, but to *proclaim* it.

This is the message of the *Mechilta:*

אִם תִּזְכּוּ לִשְׁמוֹר אֶת הַשַּׁבָּת עָתִיד הקב״ה לָתֵת לָכֶם ג׳
מוֹעֲדִים, פֶּסַח, וְעֲצֶרֶת, וְסוּכּוֹת.

If you merit to observe the Sabbath, the Holy One, Blessed is He, will give you three festivals: Passover, Shavuos, and Succos (Mechilta B'shallach 16).

Sabbath and Redemption

There is another outgrowth of the perceptions induced by the Sabbath. The Sage teach that the final Redemption can be brought by the scrupulous observance of the Sabbath. [This theme is alluded to in many of the *zemiros*, particularly in *Melaveh Malkah.*] True, גָּלוּת, *exile*, particularly the cruelty and oppression so frequently associated with it, is a physical phenomenon. Like all such phenomena in the life of Israel, however, it is but an outward manifestation of a spiritual defi-

At root, exile is a lack of awareness of God's Presence — to the extent that we perceive Him, we are with Him.

ciency. At root, exile is a lack of awareness of God's Presence — to the extent that we perceive Him, we are with Him; to the extent that we fail to recognize His omnipresence, we are exiled from Him. The determining factor is not geographical, but spiritual. [See Overview to *Megillas Esther.*] The Sabbath is the day that demands knowledge of God and His scheme, and it is the day whose holiness makes possible such knowledge to a degree unattainable during the other six days.

After God's Presence is perceived as a reality, the distance separating Israel from Him is closed. Then the barriers of physical exile will disappear of themselves.

How logical, therefore, that Sabbath observance can bring the Redemption. When the day is filled with a true awareness of what it represents — that God is the Creator and that His will is the soul of creation — then the ultimate *spiritual* redemption is already at hand. After God's Presence is perceived as a reality, the distance separating Israel from Him is closed. Then the barriers of physical exile will disappear of themselves.

III. Semblance of the World to Come

A Glimpse S*fas Emes* (to *Psalms* 92:1) cites *Toras Kohanim* that God declares to Israel, אִם אַתֶּם קְדוֹשִׁים מַעֲלֶה אֲנִי עֲלֵיכֶם כְּאִילוּ קִדַּשְׁתֶּם אֹתִי, *if you are holy, I shall consider it as though you made Me holy.* Of course, God's absolute holiness is not created by Israel, nor is it dependent upon Israel. But in the so-called here-and-now, His holiness is not apparent, and His judgments are ח"ו questioned. Israel's destiny is irrevocably intertwined with Godliness — כִּי חֵלֶק ה' עַמּוֹ, *for His nation is the portion of HASHEM* (*Deuteronomy* 32:9). If Israel raises itself and strives mightily, it can bring its attachment to God even into its earthly life. When that happens, it can perceive and even reveal God's holiness on earth. Certainly we can never understand the full measure of His holiness and His ways; even Moses could not achieve that — but it *can* achieve at least a glimpse of the World to Come here on earth.

If Israel raises itself and strives mightily, it can bring its attachment to God even into its earthly life.

That achievement is מֵעֵין עוֹלָם הַבָּא, *a semblance of the World to Come.* It is no mean feat to pull a bit of heaven down to earth, but Israel is capable of doing so, and the time most conducive for it is the Sabbath. The Sabbath day is a semblance of the World to Come (*Berachos* 57b) because it introduces a higher degree of holiness into the world below.

The Sabbath day is a semblance of the World to Come because it introduces a higher degree of holiness into the world below.

The psalm of the Sabbath, *Psalm* 92, gives us an insight into this quality of the day. Except for the introductory verse that described it as the Sabbath psalm, there is no mention of the day anywhere in all its sixteen verses. It speaks of the goodness of praising God even in the dark night of exile. It calls for praise of His great deeds even when the wicked are ascendant and the righteous downtrodden. It assures us that the good fortune of the wicked is but a prelude to their disaster, and that the travail of the righteous will give way to blossoming good fortune and exultant declarations of God's justice and fairness. Beautiful sentiments all — but where is there mention of the Sabbath and why was such a psalm chosen rather than one that speaks of the creation of heaven and earth?

The Psalm of Faith In truth, however, the psalm is ideally suited to what the day represents. The Sabbath is the day when God reveals Himself, ever so slightly perhaps, but if the individual Jew allows himself to be catapulted toward successively higher spiritual heights Sabbath after Sabbath, who can tell how brilliant his *personal* semblance of heavenly majesty will be? 'World to Come' is not an absolute concept like a specific geographical location on earth. An inhabitant of the Jordan Valley cannot ski and a dweller on Mount Everest cannot stroll along a river bank. Each place on earth is whatever it is. But the World to Come is a spiritual concept, and every Jew fashions a personal world which will reflect his attainments on earth. The Sabbath reflection of that higher world, too, mirrors the spiritual level of each individual. For some, spiritual doors open wide, enabling them to perceive God's glory on earth. They understand — or they believe with perfect faith — that His Providence is totally just.

The World to Come is a spiritual concept, and every Jew fashions a personal world which will reflect his attainments on earth.

When He smiles at us, we rejoice in the telling: לְהַגִּיד בַּבֹּקֶר חַסְדֶּךָ, *to tell of His kindness in the dawn* of good fortune and the illuminating glow of His benign countenance (v. 3). When He is angry with us and casts us away from His kind light, we are sustained by our faith: וֶאֱמוּנָתְךָ בַּלֵּילוֹת, *and in the nights [of exile and suffering, we tell] of Your faithfulness* (ibid.). Our belief in God is not dependent on His compliance with our wishes. Though we may not understand, we still have faith — and perfect faith is no less exalted than comprehension. Sometimes it is better, because there are times in life when neither history, nor experience, nor logic can sustain us. At such times, we are sustained by faith.

Perfect faith is no less exalted than comprehension. Sometimes it is better.

This is the message of the psalm. The Sabbath is here. If you strive enough and believe enough, you can perceive a *semblance* of His greatness. Let that glimpse give you strength and courage throughout the grim, unforgiving week. On the Sabbath you see a glimmer of the truth. Do not forget it as the week winds on. The more of the Sabbath you cling to, the higher the rung on which you will be standing when the next semblance of the World to Come arrives — and the better you will see (*Sfas Emes*).

Song of Kingship The seven days of the week have been likened to the seven *Sefiros*, representing the successive stages in the development of God's will, from His ineffable grandeur to a form that is perceptible on earth. The final *Sefirah* is מַלְכוּת, *kingship*. The king, as ruler, represents the public manifestation of authority. Problems are discussed and policies hammered out in privy councils, but decrees enter the public domain when they are promulgated by the power of government. The Sabbath is the time when God's glory becomes visible on earth; it is the culmination of the process by which He brings His glory from the highest sphere to ours.

The Sabbath is the time when God's glory becomes visible on earth.

The classic works speak of שִׁבְעַת הָרוֹעִים, the *Seven Shepherds*, who guided and shaped Israel's destiny: Abraham, Isaac, Jacob, Moses, Aaron, Joseph, and David. The last of the seven is King David. He, too, is מַלְכוּת, *kingship*, the human representation of God's majesty [see Overview to *Ruth*].

God's culminating manifestation on earth is thus represented by His day, the Sabbath, and His king, David. שִׁירָה, *song*, is an expression of awareness and recognition of the essential harmony of creation. It is found in the Scripture at those rare moments when the perfection of God's work was perceived [see Overview to *Shir HaShirim*]. Song is מַלְכוּת, *kingship*. David, the king, was נְעִים זְמִירוֹת יִשְׂרָאֵל, *the sweet singer of Israel*. His song was neither separate from, nor contradictory to, his kingship. To the contrary, his song was an expression of his regal mission to make known the perfection of God's work.

שִׁירָה, song, is an expression of awareness and recognition of the essential harmony of creation.

The Sabbath has the same regal mission.

וְיוֹם הַשְּׁבִיעִי מְשַׁבֵּחַ וְאוֹמֵר: מִזְמוֹר שִׁיר לְיוֹם הַשַּׁבָּת טוֹב לְהוֹדוֹת לַה׳.

The seventh day [itself] sings praise and says, This is a psalm, a song for the Sabbath day: it is good to sing praise to HASHEM (Sabbath Shacharis.

See *Otzar HaTefillos, Avodas Yisrael,* and *Siddur Siach Yitzchak* for Midrashic sources of this interpretation).

It is not only Jews who sing on the Sabbath. The initiative is taken by the day itself. It sings. It is not only Jews who sing on the Sabbath. The initiative is taken by the day itself. *It* sings, because its very essence is the expression of God's perceived Presence, a semblance of the World to Come.

Therefore Israel sings, for Israel is the echo and the mate of the Holy Sabbath.

אָשִׁירָה לַה׳ בְּחַיָּי אֲזַמְּרָה לֵאלֹהַי בְּעוֹדִי יֶעֱרַב עָלָיו שִׂיחִי אָנֹכִי אֶשְׂמַח בַּה׳.

I shall sing to HASHEM while I live, I shall give praise to my God while I exist. May my utterance be sweet to Him! I shall rejoice with HASHEM (Psalms 104:33-34).

Rabbi Nosson Scherman

"I remember once spending Shabbos with a poor working man in Williamsburg. He was a simple but pious man who did not have very much in the way of worldly goods. Seeing his cramped, dreary apartment, you would be apt to have pity on him.

"But at his Shabbos table, the man sat like a king. And he made a remark that has remained with me all these years:

" 'I pity people who don't keep Shabbos. I really pity them. They don't know what they are missing. They have no idea at all.' "

(R' Aryeh Kaplan)

Fundament of Faith

A Crucial Limb

◆§ The *mitzvah* of Shabbos is the fourth of the Ten Commandments. Of all the rituals of Judaism, Shabbos is the only one included among the Ten Commandments. It is also repeated more often in the Torah than any other *mitzvah*. Moreover, while the admonishments found in the Books of the Prophets rarely mention specific rituals, Shabbos is mentioned in the reproofs of Isaiah, Jeremiah, and Ezekiel.

In his preface to the third volume of *Mishnah Berurah*, the one dealing with the laws of Shabbos, the Chofetz Chaim writes:

"The Torah states: *Remember the Sabbath day to sanctify it. . .for in six days, Hashem made the heavens and the earth. . . (Exodus* 20:8,11). The Torah is telling us that Shabbos is a fundament of Jewish faith, for it makes known that the universe is a creation. Since God is Creator of all, He is therefore Master over all, and we are His servants and are obligated to do His will and to serve Him with our entire body, soul and resources — for all belongs to Him. Twelve times does the Torah admonish us to keep the Shabbos. Our Sages have taught: *Whoever observes the Shabbos is considered as if he has kept the entire Torah, and whoever desecrates the Shabbos is considered as if he has denied the entire Torah* — for, as we have said, Shabbos is a fundament of Jewish belief.

"One should know that the two hundred and forty-eight positive commandments, which God obligated us to remember and keep, correspond to the two hundred and forty-eight limbs in the human body. Now, the human body is comprised of a variety of limbs; certain limbs are not crucial to sustain life. While losing a hand or foot is an exceedingly great loss, nevertheless, man can survive such a loss. However, man cannot survive without his head, or with a heart that has been damaged beyond repair, for the source of life stems from these limbs.

"So it is with *mitzvos*, regarding which it is written, . . .*that man shall carry them out and by which he shall live (Leviticus* 18:5), and . . . *it is your life and the length of your days (Deuteronomy* 30:20), and other verses which teach us that one's existence in the World to Come hinges on his observance of Torah [in this world]. . .Failure to observe those *mitzvos* which correspond to the mind and heart causes the soul's primary source of vitality to be lost. Belief in God and His Torah, and the observance of Shabbos which is a fundament of faith, are the very lifeblood of the soul's existence both in this world and the Hereafter."

An Eternal Sign

בֵּינִי וּבֵין בְּנֵי יִשְׂרָאֵל אוֹת הִיא לְעֹלָם

Between Me and the Children of Israel it [the Shabbos] is an eternal sign (Exodus 31:17).

◆§ *Rambam* (*Hilchos Shabbos* 30:15) states: "The Shabbos and [the prohibition against] idol worship are each equivalent to all other *mitzvos* combined. Shabbos is the sign between the Holy One and ourselves forever. Therefore, one who transgresses any other *mitzvah* is counted among the sinners of Israel; however, one who publicly violates the Shabbos is like an idol worshiper."

To explain this, the Chofetz Chaim offered the following parable: When a store that has been open regularly is one day found to be closed, people assume that the closing is only temporary; the store is still in business. Even when they peer through the window and see the storekeeper removing the merchandise from the store's shelves, they still maintain the possibility that the store will one day reopen. However, when the sign above the store is taken down, there can be no doubt. The store is closed for good.

Said the Chofetz Chaim: If a person fails to keep any other *mitzvah*, then his 'store' of belief is still in existence, although he has abandoned it for the moment. Shabbos, however, is different. Observance of Shabbos is the confirmation of our belief in God as Creator of all things and as the One Whose statutes must shape and direct our lives. It is the 'sign' that demonstrates our faith in and allegiance to Him. To violate Shabbos is to remove that sign.

Tranquility Through Trust

שֵׁשֶׁת יָמִים תֵּעָשֶׂה מְלָאכָה וּבַיּוֹם הַשְּׁבִיעִי יִהְיֶה לָכֶם קֹדֶשׁ שַׁבַּת שַׁבָּתוֹן לַה'

For six days your work shall be done and on the seventh day it shall be hallowed for you, a complete rest for HASHEM (Exodus 35:2).

◆§ The Sages teach (*Beitzah* 16b) that the yearly earnings of each individual are decreed in Heaven on Rosh Hashanah. Nothing in the world can help a person earn one cent more than what has been decreed for him for the coming year. Though man is not to rely on miracles and must engage in some sort of *hishtadlus* [effort] to provide for his and his family's needs, he must not adopt the approach that "*my strength and the power of my hand has amassed for me this fortune*" (*Deuteronomy* 8:17). Rather, all is from God.

True *bitachon* [trust] is synonymous with true tranquility and this is especially true of the tranquility that one can and should experience on Shabbos. A person who lacks proper *bitachon* will, at the very least, find it difficult not to think about his business-related activities on Shabbos since he feels that he is in control of his material well-being. Not so the man whose trust in God is unwavering.[1]

R' Shlomo Ganzfried (in *Sefer Aperion*) finds an allusion to this in the verse stating that for six days תֵּעָשֶׂה מְלָאכָה, *your work should be done*. The word מְלָאכָה can homiletically be translated *possessions* as in אִם לֹא שָׁלַח יָדוֹ בִּמְלֶאכֶת רֵעֵהוּ, *that he did not make use of the possession of his neighbor* (*Exodus* 22:10). The word תֵּעָשֶׂה, *should be done*, as opposed to תַּעֲשֶׂה, *you shall do*, implies that, in fact, it is not one's own effort that brings him his possessions; rather, all is done for him by the One Above. Those who live by this precept will merit the second half of the verse: *and the seventh day shall be hallowed for you, a day of complete rest for Hashem*.

A similar theme is sounded by R' Moshe Feinstein (*Dorash Moshe*) regarding the verse, "Six days you shall work and the seventh day you shall rest" (*Exodus* 34:21). Why, asks R' Moshe, must the Torah mention the work of the six weekdays? The verse could have read simply, "On the seventh day you shall rest." R' Moshe resolves this by citing the teaching (*Chullin* 7b) that a person does not even bruise his finger on this world unless it has been so decreed Above. Nothing is outside the realm of Providence. Moreover, God renews creation every day and man's strength to work each day is derived from that day's renewal. As we say in the *Shacharis* prayers, "He renews in His goodness, each day, perpetually, the workings of creation." Thus, all man's work during the six weekdays is possible only because such is the will of God. This is the intent of the above verse: Both your work during the six weekdays and your rest on the seventh day are

---

1. The Ten Commandments state, "Six days you are to work and accomplish all your tasks, but the seventh day is Shabbos to HASHEM" *(Exodus* 20:9-10). *Rashi* (citing *Mechilta*) interprets: " *Six days you are to work* — When Shabbos comes it should be in your eyes as if all your work has been completed; you should not give thought to your work." Fulfillment of this dictum will depend on the level of one's trust.

because of Divine command. R' Moshe concludes that internalizing this concept will strengthen one's faith and will help him overcome any sort of hindrance with regard to *mitzvah* performance, especially that of Shabbos.

Learning the Hard Way

◄§ The Chofetz Chaim once visited the town of Chernukov, Russia where there lived a Jew whose factory operated on Shabbos. The Chofetz Chaim sent for the man and attempted to persuade him to cease working on the seventh day. The man would not agree. He said, "My factory's daily production is worth some four thousand rubles. Do you expect me to give this up every single week?!"

The Chofetz Chaim replied, "In the Torah we read: *Six days your work shall be done and the seventh day shall be hallowed*. Now, why must the Torah mention the six weekdays; would it not be sufficient to state simply that the seventh day is Shabbos? The answer, my friend, is that the success of one's labor during the six weekdays is contingent upon his sanctifying the seventh day unto God. One who desecrates the Shabbos may, due to that sin alone, forfeit his earnings of the rest of the week."

The man scoffed at the *tzaddik's* words. "Come now," he retorted. "You don't mean to tell me that my factory can be silenced by a sentence in the Torah?!"

Some time later, the Chofetz Chaim received a letter from the man. He no longer owned a factory; the government had found reason to take it from him. He had been reduced to poverty. The man wrote, "I have learned the hard way that, yes, a single sentence in the Torah has the power to silence an entire factory" (*Darchei Mussar*).

When the nineteenth-century giant R' Akiva Eiger was *Rav* in the city of Friedland (Prussia), a fire swept through the city's Jewish section, destroying many homes. When the victims went about the task of rebuilding, R' Akiva Eiger issued an announcement reminding everyone that it is rabbinically prohibited for a gentile to perform work on Shabbos for a Jew's benefit. This announcement was important because all the builders were gentiles and contractors would routinely demand that Jewish customers compensate them if their workers would not be allowed to work on the seventh day.

Everyone adhered to the *Rav's* directives — that is, everyone except for one man. He was one of the community's wealthiest and most influential personages. He did not understand this law of a gentile not doing work, and he did not want to suffer any loss of money because of it. The man therefore ignored R' Akiva Eiger's edict, confident that his personal power in the community placed him outside the Rav's jurisdiction.

Over the next few weeks, R' Akiva Eiger issued a number of public warnings regarding the matter, each warning more forceful than the previous one. However, his words succeeded only in angering the man. Finally, R' Akiva Eiger stood at the pulpit of the city's main synagogue one Shabbos and announced, "Whoever allows his house to be built on Shabbos will not enjoy his house for long." This warning, too, was ignored.

The man's house was completed. It was a magnificent edifice, a veritable palace, a landmark in the community.

Shortly after the man moved into his house, one of the roof's supporting beams collapsed. Those who examined the fallen beam were horrified to find its inside swarming with worms and badly decayed. Inspectors soon discovered that the same was true of virtually all the wood used in the house's construction. They advised that the house be vacated immediately. It was, and shortly thereafter, it collapsed into a heap of rubble.

It was obvious that this was no accident. The wood from which the house had been built was cut from the same forest of trees used for the other new homes — which were all in perfect condition.

The man was, of course, deeply shaken. He eventually rebuilt his home, though not on Shabbos. When the house was finally completed, the man was afraid that were he to live in it, it might collapse again. He therefore sold it and moved somewhere else (L'Ch'vod Shabbos).

Cheating Oneself

◆§ With regard to those who, God forbid, desecrate the Shabbos to pursue their livelihood, the Chofetz Chaim offered a parable:

A farmer was selling bushels of wheat to a merchant. To keep an exact count of the bushels sold, the merchant would throw a coin into a bowl as each bushel was placed upon his wagon. When the loading would be completed, the coins would be counted up and the total multiplied by the price per bushel.

As the loading proceeded, the ignorant farmer could not take his eyes off the gleaming coins in the bowl. How he wished that the coins were his own! He could not restrain himself. When the merchant turned his back, the farmer reached into the bowl and pocketed a few coins. What the farmer failed to realize was that the fewer coins in the bowl, the fewer bushels he would be paid for. The price per bushel far exceeded the value of each coin.

The farmer was cheating himself. And so do those who work on Shabbos.

Go to the Source

⋙ Rabbi Shmuel Greineman was present when, on a visit to the city of Vilna, the Chofetz Chaim was besieged by scores of Jews who sought his blessing. All received the blessings they requested — except for one man who had never before met the *tzaddik* from Radin. To this man, the Chofetz Chaim said, "You seek my blessing? Do you think that I am the source of blessing?" The man pleaded again and again, only to receive the same response each time.

Finally the man asked Rabbi Greineman to intercede on his behalf. The Chofetz Chaim told Rabbi Greineman, "You must explain to the man that as long as he is guilty of *chillul Shabbos*, all the blessings in the world will do him no good." For, as we say in the Friday night *Lecha Dodi* : לִקְרַאת שַׁבָּת לְכוּ וְנֵלְכָה כִּי הִיא מְקוֹר הַבְּרָכָה, *To welcome the Shabbos, come let us go, for it is the source of blessing.*

The man burst into tears. It was true, he said. He owned a flour mill which he operated seven days a week. He was shaken by the Chofetz Chaim's prophetic awareness of this fact and he promised to faithfully observe Shabbos from then on. The Chofetz Chaim then conferred his blessings (*Chofetz Chaim al HaTorah*).[1]

---

1. In a similar incident, the Chofetz Chaim told his petitioner, "It is not enough that *you* observe Shabbos. Does the Torah then tell us, 'Do not cook meat with milk, you and your son and daughter'? Does the Torah say, 'Place *tefillin* upon your head and hand, you and your son'? No, it is only with regard to Shabbos that the Torah specifically adjures us, *You may do no work — you, your son, your daughter* (*Exodus* 20:10).

"As long as your children violate the Shabbos — your son by driving and your daughter by combing her hair — it is impossible for you to receive the blessing that flows from this holy day."

The man confessed to his children's misdeeds and promised that he would see to it that they mend their ways, after which the Chofetz Chaim blessed him as he desired.

Epitome of Love

In Search of a Mate

*R' Shimon bar Yachai said: The Shabbos came before God
and said, 'Master of the universe, for each day of the week
there is a mate [Sunday and Monday, Tuesday and Wednes-
day, etc.], but I have no mate.'*

God replied, 'The Nation of Israel will be your mate'
(Bereishis Rabbah 11:8).

◆§ Shabbos represents the pinnacle of *dveikus* [attachment to God]; to
the degree that one attaches himself to the Shabbos, he attaches
himself to the One Above. For this reason, says *Ramban*, the *Mussaf*
offering of Shabbos — as opposed to that of *Yom Tov* — contained
no sin-offering, "...For on Shabbos, the Jewish Nation is בַּת זוּגוּ, *His
mate*" (*Ramban, Numbers* 28:2). *Love covers over all iniquities*
(*Proverbs* 10:12).

The 613 *mitzvos* are essentially varying means through which one
attains attachment to God. In this sense, Shabbos is the soul of all the
mitzvos and comparable to all of them combined (*Nesivos Shalom*).

An Unparalleled, Precious Gift

◆§ *At the time the Torah was given, the Holy One said to Israel: "My
children: I have an unparalleled gift that I will give you to keep forever
if you will accept My Torah and observe My mitzvos."*

The Children of Israel asked: "What is this precious gift?"

The Holy One responded: "This is the World to Come."

*Responded the Children of Israel: "Show us a semblance of the
World to Come!"*

*Said the Holy One: "The Shabbos is one-sixtieth of the World to
Come, a world that is an everlasting Shabbos"* (*Osios R' Akiva*).

*The Holy One said to Moses: "I have a precious gift hidden in My
treasure house. Its name is Shabbos and it is My desire that Israel be
granted it. Go inform them of this"* (*Beitzah 16a*).

God did not remove the Shabbos from His treasure house. Rather,
a Jew who keeps the Shabbos is lifted above his earthly existence of
the weekdays and is ushered into the treasure house itself — a
semblance of the World to Come (*Ohr Gedalyahu*).

Recognizing Its Value

❧ The door of R' Shmel'ke of Nikolsburg was forever open to those in need, even when this meant depriving himself of his own needs. Once, when a poor man appeared at R' Shmel'ke's door, the *tzaddik* could not find even a cent to give him. Looking about frantically, R' Shmel'ke spotted his wife's gold ring. Without a moment's hesitation, he handed the ring to the poor man who, of course, was overjoyed.

When R' Shmel'ke's wife came home, he immediately told her what had transpired. His wife exclaimed, "Oh no! That poor man has no idea how expensive the ring is. Some crook may come along and buy the ring from him for far less that its actual value." R' Shmel'ke agreed with his wife and hurried from the house. After a chase that lasted for some time, he finally caught up to the fellow and told him the price of the ring.

The following Friday night, R' Shmel'ke related the incident to his *chassidim*. He continued, "This is what God meant when He told Moses to inform the Jews of the precious gift of Shabbos. Moses was to convey to them the pricelessness of Shabbos, that it is a day of limitless spiritual potential. Otherwise, they might trade it away for nothing more than a piece of *kugel!"* (*Kedushas HaShabbos*).[1]

Most Coveted of Days

❧ In both the *Shemoneh Esrei* of Shabbos and the daytime *zemiros,* reference is made to God's calling the Shabbos חֶמְדַּת יָמִים, 'most coveted of days.' However, as the commentators note, there is no such Scriptural reference to the Shabbos. The commentators offer a variety of explanations:

— *Talmud Yerushalmi* translates וַיְכַל אֱלֹקִים בַּיּוֹם הַשְּׁבִיעִי, *And God coveted* [וְחַמִידָה] *the seventh day (Genesis 2:2).* [This is in contrast to the generally accepted translation *and God finished. . .*] Accordingly, at the very moment of its creation, the Shabbos is referred to as *God's most coveted day (Abudraham).*

— The reference is not Scriptural but descriptive. All heavenly and earthly blessings are dependent on the Shabbos (*Zohar*). Whatever a person does on this holy day absorbs its blessings and the influence

---

1. By Rabbi Y.P. Feldman (Jerusalem 1988). A work by Rabbi Dovid Sputz under the same title was published in New York this year.

carries over into the other days of the week. Therefore, all other days love the Shabbos because they recognize that their own success depends on the Shabbos (*Ohel Yaakov*).

Another explanation might be suggested. The phrase from the *Shemoneh Esrei* חֶמְדַּת יָמִים אוֹתוֹ קָרָאתָ, commonly interpreted *'Most coveted of days' You called it*, can also be interpreted *'Most coveted of days' You summoned it* (see *Rashbam* to *Genesis* 49:1). Shabbos is a day especially conducive for Torah study; in fact, *Tanna D'vei Eliyahu* refers to the Torah as the בֶּן זוּג, *mate*, of the Shabbos (see page 85). Torah is called כְּלִי חֶמְדָּה, *a coveted utensil* (*Avos* 3:18). Thus is the day which was 'summoned' for Torah study referred to as a חֶמְדַּת יָמִים.

Shabbos and the Exodus

Complementary Concepts

> *Blessed are You, HASHEM. . .Who with love and favor gave us His holy Shabbos as a heritage, a remembrance of creation . . . a memorial of the Exodus from Egypt (Shabbos Eve Kiddush).*

◄§ In the first version of the Ten Commandments (*Exodus* 20:11), Shabbos is described as a symbol of God's creation of the universe. However, In the Torah's repetition of the Commandments, the redemption from Egypt is given as the reason for the *mitzvah* of Shabbos: "And you shall remember that you were slaves in the land of Egypt and HASHEM your God took you from there with a mighty hand and an outstretched arm. Therefore, HASHEM, your God, commanded you to make this day of Shabbos" (*Deuteronomy* 5:15).

Ramban (*Deuteronomy* 5:15) explains that the two concepts are intertwined. Shabbos *is* symbolic of creation. However, it was the Exodus which demonstrated to humanity that God controls all of nature, directing it as He sees fit. Thus, the events of the Exodus bear witness to that which the Shabbos represents, while the testimony of Shabbos observance brings to mind the Redemption. As *Ramban* puts it, "The Shabbos is a remembrance of the Exodus, while the Exodus is a remembrance of the Shabbos."

A Fitting Partner

◄§ On a deeper level, *S'fas Emes* cites the *Midrash* (quoted above) that Shabbos could find no partner in creation until God granted it the Jewish Nation as a mate. That Shabbos could not be joined with any other item in creation is because it is of another world entirely, a *semblance of the World to Come* (*Berachos* 57b). How can creatures of this mundane earth have any sort of attachment to a day that is so spiritual, so sublime? Only the Jewish Nation, who endured the purifying process of the Egyptian exile until departing that land as God's Chosen People, who attained a heightened level of holiness and purity as they witnessed God's miracles at the Splitting of the Sea — only such a nation can truly experience and attach itself to the day of Shabbos.

Shabbos and the Manna

The Manna's Lesson

◄§ During the Jews' forty-year sojourn in the Wilderness, their nourishment came from the manna, the miraculous sustenance which fell from Heaven each day. On Friday a double portion of manna fell in honor of Shabbos, on which none fell.

There is a profound relationship between Shabbos and the manna. In the verse where Moses instructs the Jews to eat Friday's extra portion on Shabbos, the word הַיּוֹם, *today*, appears three times (*Exodus* 16:25). From here the Sages derive that three meals should be eaten on Shabbos (*Shabbos* 117b).

The manna is symbolized at each Shabbos meal by the *lechem mishneh*, two loaves, with which each meal is begun. This is a remembrance of the double portion of manna that fell on Friday. The Shabbos tablecloth represents the dew that covered the ground before the manna fell and the '*challah* cover' on top is symbolic of the second dew that fell atop the manna to protect it (*Tur, Orach Chaim* 271:12).

The forty-year sojourn in the Wilderness was a totally spiritual experience. The Jews ate manna, drank from the miraculous well of

Miriam, and were protected by the Clouds of Glory. The lessons of that time were meant for future generations as well. As the Torah states: "And He fed you the manna that neither you nor your fathers had known — to teach you that man does not survive by bread alone; rather, through the word of God does man live" (*Deuteronomy* 8:3).

Thus the lesson of the manna is one of fundamental *emunah* and *bitachon*, faith and trust, which the day of Shabbos — a remembrance of creation and the Exodus from Egypt — represents.

A Blessing for All Time

וַיְבָרֶךְ אֱלֹקִים אֶת יוֹם הַשְּׁבִיעִי וַיְקַדֵּשׁ אֹתוֹ. . .

God blessed the seventh day and hallowed it (Genesis 2:3):

He blessed — for all week long one portion of manna per person fell, but on Friday a double portion fell.

And hallowed it — through the manna, which did not fall on Shabbos (Rashi).

◈§ *Rashi's* comment requires explanation. Why, in the chapter of Creation, should reference be made to a blessing and sanctity which was granted to a single generation — that of the Wilderness?

R' Moshe Shternbuch *(Ta'am V'daas)* explains that the generation which ate the manna experienced the epitome of restful contentment on Shabbos. Their Shabbos needs were granted them every Friday morning with the double portion of manna, they did not have any manna to collect on Shabbos itself, and they had no need to give thought on Shabbos to their work in the days ahead because there was no work at all! They relied entirely on God for all their needs.

The contentment which they experienced was a very special blessing indeed — and every Jew who strives to live his Shabbos in the desired manner can experience that very same feeling of contentment. Thus, the blessing of the manna is, in fact, a blessing for all generations.[1]

---

1. The *Steipler Gaon* (in *Birchas Peretz*) notes that the *gematria* (numerical value) of וַיְקַדֵּשׁ אֹתוֹ, *and He hallowed it*, plus 1 (see p. 44) is equal to בֵּרְכוֹ בַּמָּן וְקִדְּשׁוֹ בַּמָּן, *He blessed it with manna and hallowed it with manna* (728).

With regard to the prohibition against gathering the manna on Shabbos, Moses said: אַל יֵצֵא אִישׁ מִמְּקֹמוֹ בַּיּוֹם הַשְּׁבִיעִי, *Let no man go out from his place on the seventh day* (*Exodus* 16:29). *Rashi* (citing *Eruvin* 51a) comments: אֵלּוּ אַלְפַּיִם אַמָּה שֶׁל תְּחוּם שַׁבָּת, *This is (an allusion to) the two thousand cubits of the Shabbos boundary* (past which one may not walk on Shabbos). The Steipler notes that the *gematria* of מִמְּקֹמוֹ, *from his place,* plus 1 is equal to that of אַלְפַּיִם אַמָּה, *two thousand cubits* (227).

For a Safekeeping

∙§ Regarding the extra portion of manna which fell on Friday, Moses told the people: הַנִּיחוּ לָכֶם לְמִשְׁמֶרֶת עַד הַבֹּקֶר, *Leave it for yourselves for a safekeeping until morning (Exodus* 16:23). Later, Moses commanded the people in the name of God that a measure of manna be stored in the *Mishkan* (Tabernacle):

מְלֹא הָעֹמֶר מִמֶּנּוּ לְדֹרֹתֵיכֶם לְמַעַן יִרְאוּ אֶת הַלֶּחֶם אֲשֶׁר הֶאֱכַלְתִּי אֶתְכֶם
בַּמִּדְבָּר בְּהוֹצִיאִי אֶתְכֶם מֵאֶרֶץ מִצְרָיִם.

Fill an omer measure with it [manna] as a safekeeping for all generations, so that they will see the bread which I fed you in the Wilderness when I took you out of the land of Egypt (ibid. v.32).

The use of the term מִשְׁמֶרֶת, *safekeeping*, for both the manna that was stored away and the manna of Shabbos, alludes to the fact that even after the manna totally vanished from our midst, its spiritual properties still remained for all generations. Hidden in the food that is prepared in every Jewish home in honor of Shabbos is a spiritual spark from the Heavenly food from which our ancestors derived nourishment more than three thousand years ago. This explains the statement (*Mechilta, Beshalach* ch.17), "Torah was given to be expounded only to those who ate from the manna." Every Jew in every generation is accorded such a status when he partakes of the Shabbos meal (*Sefer HaParshios*).

Of Another World

Sign of Eternity

∙§ *Reishis Chochmah* explains אוֹת הִיא לְעֹלָם, *it [i.e., the Shabbos] is an eternal sign (Exodus* 31:17), to mean that Shabbos is 'a sign of eternity,' for it is מֵעֵין עוֹלָם הַבָּא, *a semblance of the World to Come*.

More Than a Semblance

◄§ Rabbi Yisrael Spira, the late Bluzhever *Rebbe*, grew up in the court of his illustrious grandfather, known by the title of his famous work, *Tzvi LaTzaddik*. The highlight of the *Tzvi LaTzaddik*'s Friday night *tish* (public Shabbos meal) was the singing of *Kah Ribon* to a stirring tune that originated with the *Tzvi LaTzaddik*'s grandfather, the *Bnei Yissoschor*. On one particular week, when the *Tzvi LaTzaddik* did not conduct his *tish*, his young grandson and a friend desperately wanted to see how the *Tzvi LaTzaddik* experienced the Shabbos in the privacy of his study. They convinced the *gabbai* to leave the study door slightly ajar, so that they could watch undetected.

They beheld an awesome sight. On the table, the Shabbos candles flickered. From the ceiling hung burning oil lamps. The *Tzvi LaTzaddik* stood near the fireplace, clothed in his *bekeshe* and *shtreimel*, swaying to and fro with his eyes shut tight, as he sang *Kah Ribon* unlike any the two boys had ever heard. The *Tzvi LaTzaddik* interspersed *Yiddish* words among the Hebrew phrases of the song, as he sought to express the feelings of his soul:

לְמִקְדָּשֵׁךְ תּוּב: וואָס שַׁאט עֶס דִיר אַז עֶס וֶועט שׁוֹין זַײַן לְמִקְדָּשֵׁךְ תּוּב?
To Your sanctuary return: What loss could You possibly suffer from returning to Your sanctuary once again?

וּלְקוֹדֶשׁ קוּדְשִׁין: וֶוען וֶועט עֶס נָאךְ אַמָאל זַײַן וּלְקוֹדֶשׁ קוּדְשִׁין?
And to Your holy of holies: When will it once again be *Your holy of holies?*

אוּן וָואס וֶועט דָארְט זַײַן? וִיזַמְרוּן לָךְ שִׁירִין וְרַחֲשִׁין.
And what will transpire there? They will sing to You songs and praises.

אוּן וּוא וֶועט עֶס זַײַן? בִּירוּשְׁלֵם קַרְתָּא דְשׁוּפְרַיָּא.
And where will this transpire? In Jerusalem, city of beauty.

A noise at the door shook the *Tzvi LaTzaddik* from his rapture. At first, he scolded the boys for being where they should not have been. Than his face softened and he said: "Did you see how the *lechtelech* (candles) danced and jumped, shouting *'Shabbos Kodesh!'*? Did you notice how even the oil lamps danced and jumped: *'Shabbos' Kodesh!'*?

"Is anyone going to try and convince me that Shabbos is but a *semblance* of the World to Come? I assure you that I wish on myself no better than that which I am experiencing at this very moment."

Day of Return

אָמַר ר׳ חִיָּיא בַּר אַבָּא אָמַר ר׳ יוֹחָנָן: כָּל הַמְשַׁמֵּר שַׁבָּת כְּהִלְכָתוֹ אֲפִילוּ
עוֹבֵד עֲבוֹדָה זָרָה כְּדוֹר אֱנוֹשׁ מוֹחֲלִין לוֹ.

*R' Chiya bar Aba said in the name of R' Yochanan: Whoever
keeps Shabbos in accordance with its dictates will be forgiven
[of all his sins] even if he worships idols as in the days of
Enosh[1] (Shabbos 118b).*

Adam's Deduction

ה‏§ The power of atonement that is inherent in Shabbos was recognized
from the beginning of time. *Yalkut Shimoni* (*Genesis* 4:38) relates:

'*A psalm, a song for the seventh day'* (*Psalms* 92:1). R' Levi said: 'This
psalm was first sung by Adam. Adam encountered Cain and asked
him, "What became of the judgment against you?" Cain replied,
"I repented and was granted clemency." Striking himself on the face
[in amazement], Adam exclaimed, "The power of repentance is so
great and I did not know!" Adam immediately arose and recited this
psalm.'

Cain had murdered his brother Abel. God informed Cain that as
punishment, he, the tiller of soil, would no longer find the ground
productive; he would wander from place to place in search of fertile
land. Tranquility would elude him.

Cain viewed this punishment as a death sentence, for his
wanderings would leave him vulnerable to attack. "My iniquities are
too great to be borne!. . .I must become a vagrant and wanderer on
earth — whoever finds me will kill me" (*Genesis* 4:14). *Ramban*
understands this statement as Cain's confession. In the merit of his
repentance, Cain was granted a sign of protection and God declared
that would Cain be murdered, his death would be avenged.

Adam surely had reason to be amazed. Cain had committed murder
and the nature of his repentance did not seem commensurate with
either his sin or his own spiritual level. God communicated directly to
him and had admonished him to repent *before* he killed his brother
(ibid. vs. 6-7). Moreover, Cain's repentance was not motivated by

---

1.See *Genesis* 4:26.

love of God but by fear of retribution — ". . .whoever finds me will kill me" — the lowest level of repentance.

Yet his repentance was accepted and his life was spared. Adam took this lesson and applied it to Shabbos, whose essence inspires a *teshuvah me'ahavah*, repentance out of love, a most exalted form of repentance. Thus was he inspired to sing the praises of the seventh day (*R' Yehudah Zev Segal*).

A New Person

◆§ *Nesivos Shalom* offers another explanation for the power of atonement inherent in Shabbos. As already mentioned, the essence of Shabbos can accomplish the highest level of *dveikus*, spiritual attachment, between the Jew and his Creator. This attachment increases as the Shabbos day progresses. *Abudraham* writes that the three Shabbos *Shemoneh Esrei* prayers allude to this progression.

The fourth blessing in the Friday night *Ma'ariv* opens with אַתָּה קִדַּשְׁתָּ, *You have sanctified*, an allusion to קִדּוּשִׁין, *kiddushin*, the initial stage of the marriage process. Shabbos day is akin to the נִשּׂוּאִין, *nesuin*, the second part of the marriage process when all marital obligations take effect. The words יִשְׂמַח מֹשֶׁה, *Moses rejoiced*, in the *Shacharis* prayer allude to the joy of this bond of love. In the *Shemoneh Esrei* of *Minchah*, the words אַתָּה אֶחָד וְשִׁמְךָ אֶחָד, *You are One and Your Name is One*, allude to the יִחוּד, *unity*, between God and the Children of Israel that is accomplished as Shabbos draws to a close.

Ran (*Masechta Kiddushin*) writes that in agreeing to *kiddushin*, a woman indicates a submission of will toward her husband. On Shabbos, a Jew attains attachment to His creator by renewing his dedication to His service and submitting his will to fulfilling His desire. In doing so, one becomes like a בְּרִיָּה חֲדָשָׁה, *new person*.[1] He is not the same person as before. It is as if the sins of yesterday were committed by someone else, not himself. Thus does Shabbos have the power to atone for even the most grievous sins.

---

1. This is why a bride and groom attain atonement of all sins on their wedding day. As they prepare for a new life together, each becomes like a בְּרִיָּה חֲדָשָׁה, *new person*, and are not held responsible for past sins. *Nesivos Shalom* writes that to attain this status, both bride and groom should renew their dedication toward what should be their common goal as they begin their life together — fulfilling the will of God.

Like Soap

עַל כֵּן אֲכַבֵּס בּוֹ לִבִּי כְּבוֹרִית

*Therefore, I shall cleanse my heart in it [i.e., on the Shabbos]
like soap (Daytime Zemiros).*

◆§ The song does not say "with soap," but rather, "like soap." This is
to teach that a Jew should purify his heart on Shabbos until it
attains the quality of soap; that is, not only will it be pure but it will
have the power to purify and cleanse the hearts of others (*Divrei
Yechezkel citing R' Zvi Hirsh of Rimanov*).

Saved by the Shabbos

◆§ The crown of the city of Ishpitzin was the Chassidic *Rebbe* R'
Beirish, who was known far and wide as a *tzaddik* and miracle
worker. It was common knowledge among the religious Jews of
Ishpitzin that a crust of the *Rebbe*'s Shabbos *challah* or a bit of his
Kiddush wine, at times, provide a cure for the most dreadful
ailment.

In the city there lived a Jewish doctor whose religious observance
left much to be desired. Having been educated in *yeshivos*, the man
was quite learned and relished the opportunity to show off his
Torah knowledge in public. At the same time, he had little respect
for the Chassidic *Rebbe* and his "so-called cures," and he let his
feelings be known.

Once, the two found themselves seated on the dais at a
celebration. The *Rebbe* was accorded the honor due him, while the
doctor received far less. Angered by what he perceived as a slight
to his honor, the doctor avenged himself after this incident by
publicly ridiculing R' Beirish and his followers. The followers grew
incensed and they asked that their *Rebbe* allow them to respond in
kind. R' Beirish, however, would not hear of it. He told them, "This
man will one day mend his ways."

One day, the doctor became stricken with a severe kidney
ailment. He lay hovering near death; the medicines that were
administered accomplished nothing. He now regretted his misdeeds — especially those directed toward R' Beirish. On Shabbos,
he summoned the community's leaders to his bedside and asked
that they go to the *Rebbe* and beg forgiveness in his name. He

promised that were he to recover, he would become a sincerely devout Jew and would not repeat his past behavior.

The *Rebbe* told his visitors, "Our Sages have taught that even one who worships idols as in the days of Enosh will be forgiven of his sins if he observes the Shabbos properly. *Taz* (*Orach Chaim* 243:1) questions this teaching, for if one sincerely repents, then he should be forgiven in that merit alone; and if he does not sincerely repent, then Shabbos should not bring about his forgiveness!

"*Taz* answers that there are certain sins for which sincere *teshuvah*, repentance, is not sufficient (see *Mishnah Yoma* 8:8). However, sincere repentance coupled with proper Shabbos observance can atone for even such sins.

"Among the sins for which *teshuvah* alone does not suffice is *chillul Hashem*, desecration of God's Name. The doctor has severely transgressed the sin of *chillul Hashem* by repeatedly ridiculing those who fear God. However, he is fortunate, for today is Shabbos. If he will repent sincerely, then the power of Shabbos will bring about his atonement and he will recover."

The *Rebbe* then gave his visitors some of his *Kiddush* wine and instructed that the doctor drink it. The doctor completely recovered and became R' Beirish's loyal disciple (*L'Ch'vod Shabbos*).

Shabbos: Now and Everlasting

Song of the Day

◄§ *Psalm* 92, which opens with the words מִזְמוֹר שִׁיר לְיוֹם הַשַּׁבָּת, *A psalm, a song for the Shabbos day*, was sung by the Levites in the Temple on Shabbos and is recited as part of the Shabbos prayers.

This demands explanation, for aside from its introductory verse, the psalm contains not a single direct reference to the Shabbos. According to the *Mishnah* (*Tamid* 7:4), the psalm refers not to the weekly Shabbos, but to the יוֹם שֶׁכֻּלּוֹ שַׁבָּת, *Day of Everlasting Shabbos*, of the Messianic era. According to the *Midrash*, however, the psalm was sung by Adam in honor of the Shabbos day. *Targum Yonasan* (*Song of Songs* 1:1) counts this psalm among the ten *shiros*, songs, uttered in this world. What, then, is the essence of this song?

The answer to this, says the Brisker *Rav* (*Chiddushei HaGriz*), lies in the psalm's sixth verse: מַה גָּדְלוּ מַעֲשֶׂיךָ ה', מְאֹד עָמְקוּ מַחְשְׁבֹתֶיךָ, *How great are Your deeds, HASHEM; exceedingly profound are Your thoughts.*

One is obligated to express praise to God when witnessing any nature-related occurrence which is extraordinary and inspires awe of Heaven. Similarly, a Jew expresses praise of God every day for His constant renewal of creation: *Blessed are You, HASHEM. . .Who in His goodness renews daily, perpetually, the work of creation. How great are Your works, HASHEM, You make them all with wisdom. . .*

Of all the billions of souls who have descended to this earth since the beginning of time, no one had more reason to exult over creation than Adam. He was brought into this world on its sixth day and was witness to a universe that had just been formed. He had to offer praise, but this could not happen until creation had reached completion. The *Mishnah* (*Avos* 5:8) relates that ten items were created during twilight of the sixth day. These items came into being at the very moment when the sixth day ended and the seventh day began. Thus, it was on Shabbos that Adam offered praise — not only for the individual items that had been created, but also for the symphony of a world whose individual components functioned in perfect unison. *"How great are Your deeds, HASHEM. . ."*

The Talmud (*Avodah Zarah* 5a) relates that God showed Adam each generation and its leaders until the end of time. This means that to Adam was revealed the deep and intricate designs of Providence as it guides this world toward a course that will result in the Day of Everlasting Shabbos — at which time these designs will become clear to all. The workings of Providence are, in fact, mentioned in this psalm: *When the wicked bloom like grass and all the doers of iniquity blossom — it is to destroy them till eternity!*

Thus did Adam have a second reason to exult: *"How exceedingly profound are Your thoughts. . ."* — and thus does the song of Shabbos convey a dual message.

The message of Psalm 92 is highly relevant to the seventh day. Shabbos is a reminder of one's true purpose in life, to serve God with all his heart and soul, so that he will merit to experience the Day of Everlasting Shabbos of the future. Moreover, on Shabbos a Jew actually partakes of the future world — of the peace and sublimity of the Messianic age. It is with regard to that future era that our Sages said: *He who toiled prior to Shabbos will eat [i.e., reap reward] on Shabbos* (*Avodah Zarah* 3a).

Redemption Through Shabbos

Were Israel to observe two Sabbaths properly, they would immediately be redeemed (Shabbos 118b).

◄§ In its simple sense, 'observing two Sabbaths properly' means for Israel to attain the highest level of Shabbos observance for two consecutive weeks. Such an accomplishment would indicate the Nation's having freed itself of inner subjugation to the passions and desires of this world. A natural result of such attainment would be ultimate redemption, for a nation that has achieved total victory in life's greatest struggle — the conquering of one's evil inclination — cannot remain subjugated to the laws and whims of foreign nations (*Misod Chachamim*).[1]

Give and Take

◄§ *Michtav Me'Eliyahu* (Vol. IV, p.143) offers another explanation of the above teaching. 'Two Sabbaths' is a reference to different aspects of the Shabbos experience. There is the 'external Shabbos'; that is, the gift of spiritual blessing that flows from Above to every Jewish soul on Shabbos. This flow is an unchanging fact, and is not contingent upon the spiritual status of the Nation as a whole or on one's personal spiritual level. The 'internal Shabbos' refers to the spiritual blessing that an individual contributes to the Shabbos. There are those who enter the Shabbos in a state of spiritual readiness through which they actually enhance the day by adding to its aura. It is concerning such individuals that the *Midrash (Bereishis Rabbah* 11:9) states: "The Congregation of Israel is your [the Shabbos'] mate; זָכוֹר אֶת יוֹם הַשַּׁבָּת לְקַדְּשׁוֹ, *Remember the Shabbos day to sanctify it (Exodus* 20:8)." The *Midrash* is relating the word לְקַדְּשׁוֹ to קִדּוּשִׁין, *betrothal*. In this relationship, Israel is likened to the male (i.e., giver) and Shabbos the female (i.e., recipient).

---

1. It is in this vein that *Misod Chachamim* relates this teaching to that which precedes it: "R' Yehudah said in the name of Rav: 'Had Israel kept the first Shabbos [in the Wilderness], no nation or sect would have had dominion over it.'" As proof, Rav cites the account of Amalek's attack against Israel which occurred soon after the nation had reached such awesome heights at the Splitting of the Sea (*Exodus* 17:8). In Rav's opinion, Israel's vulnerability to physical attack was indicative of a spiritual weakness that came to light when some individuals contravened God's will by searching for manna on Shabbos (*Exodus* 16:27). Had the entire Nation kept that *first* Shabbos properly, this too would have indicated a total negation of inner earthliness, resulting in complete and ultimate redemption. (This is further elaborated upon in *Sefer Shabbos HaMalkah*.)

When the Jewish Nation will achieve a perfect synthesis of these two forces, where they will receive the Shabbos' spiritual flow, internalize it, and, in turn, affect the day with their own spirituality — then they will immediately be redeemed.

The Shabbos Aura

And He Hallowed It

וַיְבָרֶךְ אֱלֹקִים אֶת יוֹם הַשְּׁבִיעִי וַיְקַדֵּשׁ אוֹתוֹ.

God blessed the seventh day and hallowed it (Genesis 2:3).

◄§ "The sanctity of Shabbos is superior to all sanctities, and its blessing is superior to all blessings. Therefore, it was hallowed and blessed from the beginning of creation, as it is written, 'And Elokim hallowed the seventh day and sanctified it' (*Genesis* 2:3) — and it is the source of all blessing for the rest of the week. In seven sections of the Torah[1] Israel is commanded regarding Shabbos, to show that all seven days of the week revolve around Shabbos. This is why the song of each day begins with, 'Today is the. . .day of the Shabbos' " (*Aruch HaShulchan*, *Orach Chaim* 242:1).

Though *Rashi* (based on *Midrash*) understands the above verse as an allusion to future events, the plain meaning here is that God gave the Shabbos a special blessing that raised it above the vicissitudes of this world (*Ohr HaChaim*). It is a day endowed with a spiritual exaltation, a sanctity which sets it apart from all other days. The sanctity of the Shabbos is tangible and can be perceived by any Jew who truly strives to perceive it. And not only can a Jew perceive the Shabbos, but the Shabbos can also be perceived upon him. *Midrash Rabbah* (*Bereishis* 11:2) states: "A person's countenance is not the same on Shabbos as it is the rest of week.[2]"

---

1. *Parshios Beshalach, Yisro, Mishpatim, Ki Sisa, Vayakhel, Emor, Va'eschanan*.

2. During the festive week following a Jewish marriage, the *sheva berachos* blessings recited at the wedding are repeated at each meal attended by the bride and groom. On weekdays, it is necessary that one of those at the meal be a *panim chadashos* (lit. new face), i.e., one who did not participate in any of the couple's earlier meals. On Shabbos, however, this is not required. *S'fas Emes* writes that the above *Midrash*, which teaches that every Jew has, in a sense, a different countenance on Shabbos, is the source for this *halachah*.

Joy With Trepidation

◆§ *Rambam* (*Hilchos Beis HaBechirah* 6:15) rules that the sanctity with which the Temple Mount was endowed at the time of the Temple's construction remains forever. Accordingly, it is forbidden to enter the Mount nowadays in a state of *tumah*, ritual impurity (which is everyone's status today), just as it was more than two thousand years ago. Whence did this sanctity stem? *Rambam* writes: "Solomon sanctified the Temple courtyard and Jerusalem both for that time and for the future." The efforts of King Solomon caused the manifestation of a *kedushah*, sanctity, that would remain on the Temple Mount for all time.

Rambam further states (7:7): "Although, due to our sins, the Temple still lies in ruins in our time, one must treat that place with the same awe that was accorded it when the Temple stood. . .as it is written, 'You shall observe My Shabbos and you shall have awe for My sanctuary' (*Leviticus* 26:2) — Just as observance of Shabbos is eternal, so is awe of the Temple eternal; though it is destroyed, its sanctity remains."

While the Torah compares the sanctity of the Temple to that of Shabbos, there is a vast difference between the two. The Temple, as *Rambam* states, acquired its sanctity through human effort. The sanctity of Shabbos flows directly from God, Who "blessed the seventh day and hallowed it." Now, if the Torah is so concerned lest we enter the Temple area in a state of unpreparedness, or lest we behave disrespectfully when even *facing* that place — how careful must we be with regard to the sanctity of Shabbos! (*Lev Eliyahu*).

Deliyos Yechezkel explains that in a certain sense, the sanctity of Shabbos *is* attained through man's efforts. In the *Shemoneh Esrei* of Shabbos the Jewish nation is described as עַם מְקַדְּשֵׁי שְׁבִיעִי, a *people that sanctifies the seventh*. Each week, the sanctity of Shabbos is incomplete until the Jewish people recite the verses that testify to God's creation and experience the day as one of sanctity and restful contentment. This explains why a Jew who recites the chapter of וַיְכֻלּוּ הַשָּׁמַיִם[1] on the eve of Shabbos is considered a partner with God in the workings of Creation (*Shabbos* 119b). He is a partner in a very real

---

1. The concluding verses of the chapter of Creation (*Genesis* 2:1-3) which tell of God's having ceased from creating on the seventh day. These verses are recited both in the *Shemoneh Esrei* of *Ma'ariv* and in the *Kiddush* of Shabbos eve.

sense, for the sanctity generated by his Shabbos observance complements that which is intrinsic to the day. It is with regard to this capacity of the Jewish People that the *Midrash* states:

> *And now, so says* HASHEM: *"Your creator is Jacob, your molder Israel" — R' Pinchas said in the name of R' Reuven: "The Holy One said to His world: 'My world, My world: I will tell you who created you and who molded you. Jacob created you, Jacob molded you' " (Vayikra Rabbah 36:4).*

An Additional Soul

> *Reish Lakish said: On the eve of Shabbos, The Holy One, Blessed is He, grants each person a* נְשָׁמָה יְתֵרָה, *additional soul; at the conclusion of Shabbos, it is taken from him, as it is written (Exodus 31:17):* וּבַיּוֹם הַשְּׁבִיעִי] שָׁבַת וַיִּנָּפַשׁ, '*[and on the seventh day] He ceased and rested' — (Homiletically, this can be interpreted):* כֵּיוָן שֶׁשָּׁבַת, *Once he [i.e. a Jew] has rested,* then וַי אָבְדָה נֶפֶשׁ, *"Woe! The (additional) soul is lost!*[1]" *(Beitzah 16a).*

◄§ The Steipler *Gaon* (in *Birchas Peretz*) notes that the *gematria* of הַשְּׁבִיעִי שָׁבַת וַיִּנָּפַשׁ plus 1 is equal to כֵּיוָן שֶׁשָּׁבַת וַי אָבְדָה נֶפֶשׁ (1546).[2]

While the Talmudic term used here for (additional) soul is נְשָׁמָה, *neshamah*, this teaching is derived from the Scriptural word וַיִּנָּפַשׁ, whose root is נֶפֶשׁ, *nefesh*, another term meaning *soul*. *Nesivos Shalom* explains that aside from its obvious meaning, the term נֶפֶשׁ can also mean *desire* or *yearning* (see *Genesis* 23:8). Scripture often uses this term when describing an intense spiritual yearning, as in: כְּאַיָּל תַּעֲרֹג עַל אֲפִיקֵי מָיִם כֵּן נַפְשִׁי תַעֲרֹג אֵלֶיךָ אֱלֹקִים, *As the deer calls*

---

1. The commentators are troubled by the implication here that the cry of "Woe, the soul is lost!" is uttered at the *beginning* of Shabbos, rather than at its end. One solution is that those who perceive the presence of the additional soul are so uplifted by it that they immediately cringe at the thought that when Shabbos ends, the soul will take leave of them.

2. *Bnei Yissoschor* cites two Scriptural sources to prove that two sides of a *gematria* equation are considered equal even when there is a difference of 1.

The first proof is from *Deuteronomy* 4:25, where the Torah speaks of the Jewish People becoming corrupt after remaining long (וְנוֹשַׁנְתֶּם) in its Land and turning to idol worship. The next verse states that in retribution for this, *you shall soon utterly perish. . .* The Talmud (*Sanhedrin* 38a) says that God was compassionate in sending the Jews into

*longingly for the brooks of water, so does my soul call longingly to You,
O God (Psalms* 42:2). Now, everything in creation has a counter-balance; while the soul craves for the spiritual, one's נֶפֶשׁ הַבְּהֵמִית, *corporeal
being,* craves the very opposite. Thus, the term נֶפֶשׁ is also used in reference to the most base physical desires (see *Genesis* 34:8).

With the onset of Shabbos, a Jew experiences a tremendous spiritual awakening. His earthly being is diminished, and his Heavenly soul yearns to be close to its Creator, to delight with the Source whence it came. This awakening is unique to the day of Shabbos and it is this uplifting of the soul which is the essence of the *neshamah yeseirah*, additional soul.

Nesivos Shalom continues that it is with this in mind that our Sages instituted the Friday night recitation of the passage from *Exodus* (31:16-17) in which the word וַיִּנָּפַשׁ appears. As Shabbos begins, a Jew should be cognizant of the enormous spiritual opportunities that Shabbos brings with it. If utilized properly, each succeeding Shabbos can bring one to a higher spiritual level, to a closeness with God and attachment to Torah that will remain with him long after his additional soul has left. For those who experience the day in this way, Shabbos is truly a בְּרִית עוֹלָם, *eternal covenant* (ibid.), for its lofty effects remain with them forever.

Even the Ignorant

◆§ According to Torah law, produce of the Land of Israel may not be consumed until it has been properly tithed. With the passage of time, the Sages realized that many *amei ha'aretz*, ignorant people, were becoming less scrupulous in their observance of these laws and could not be trusted regarding tithing. The Sages therefore required a buyer to separate certain tithes before consuming any produce bought from an *am ha'aretz*.

---

exile 850 years after they entered the Land of Israel, for had they been in the Land for 852 years — the *gematria* of וְנוֹשַׁנְתֶּם — the prophesied curse . . . *you will soon utterly perish. . .* would have been fulfilled in all its harshness. It is apparent from this statement that were the Jews to have been exiled after 851 years, one less than the value of וְנוֹשַׁנְתֶּם, they would have still been liable to incur the full punishment of that verse.

The second proof is where Jacob told Joseph אֶפְרַיִם וּמְנַשֶּׁה כִּרְאוּבֵן וְשִׁמְעוֹן יִהְיוּ לִי, *Ephraim and Manasseh shall be to me like Reuben and Simeon (Genesis* 48:5). The plain meaning is·that Joseph's two sons would have the status of tribes and be considered equals to Reuben and Simeon (the oldest of Jabob's sons). *Baal HaTurim* notes that this status is alluded to in the numerical equivalency of אֶפְרַיִם וּמְנַשֶּׁה to שִׁמְעוֹן וְשִׁמְעוֹן. In fact, the *gematria* of אֶפְרַיִם וּמְנַשֶּׁה is 732, while that of רְאוּבֵן וְשִׁמְעוֹן is 731.

Talmud Yerushalmi (D'mai ch.4) offers an exception to the above: "On Shabbos, the *am ha'aretz* is trusted with regard to tithes, *for the awe of Shabbos is upon him and he speaks truth.* "

Divrei Emunah explains:

> "The sanctity of Shabbos arouses a person from the slumber which the vanities of this world bring upon him throughout the week. It illuminates within him the wisdom to perceive that all the physical pleasures of the world are nothing but emptiness, and that what is important is that one attach himself to the One and Only Living God. Therefore, even the ignorant are trusted on Shabbos, for the awe of Shabbos is upon them, and they too are aroused on the holy Shabbos, each in accordance with his own spiritual level.
>
> "In earlier times, there were *tzaddikim* who yearned ceaselessly for Shabbos; as soon as one Shabbos ended, they were already yearning for the next one. On Shabbos itself, the sanctity of the day burned within them like a flaming fire, as they cried out from the depths of their hearts, '*Heiliger Shabbos'* ('Hallowed Shabbos')! They found it virtually impossible to sleep on Shabbos eve, because of the sacred fire within them. The Sanzer *Rav* likened this to a king who slept little every night. The king explained, 'I don't want to slumber through my reign, for when I sleep I am not a king — I am no different from any other slumbering soul.' Every moment of Shabbos, said the Sanzer, is too precious to sleep through."

Day of Truth

⋙ That even the ignorant find it impossible to lie on Shabbos may also be due to the profound relationship between Shabbos and the attribute of truth. This relationship is alluded to in that the *mispar katan* (digit sum) of both שַׁבָּת, *Shabbos*, and אֱמֶת, *emes*, equals 9.

ש=300 3+0+0=3 ב=2 ת=400 4+0+0=4 3+2+4=9
א=1 מ=40 4+0=4 ת=400 4+0+0=4 1+4+4=9

The number 9 is itself unique in that no matter how many times it is multiplied, the digit sum does not change: It always equals 9.

[9x2 = 18 1 + 8 = 9   9x3 = 27 2 + 7 = 9   9x4 = 36 3 + 6 = 9
9x5 = 45 4 + 5 = 9 9x6 = 54 5 + 4 = 8 + 9. . .]

אֱמֶת, *truth,* is unchanging. On Shabbos, a Jew takes note of the unchanging truths of God's existence, of His eternal Presence and Providence, and of man's true purpose in this world.

Yochanan ben Torta

ᴥ§ *Pesikta Rabbasi* (14:2) tells the story of an *animal* that was affected by the sanctity of Shabbos:

> *Our Sages related: It happened once that a Jew owned a cow that plowed. The Jew's fortunes plummeted, and he was forced to sell the cow to a gentile. The cow worked for the gentile for six days, but on Shabbos it sat down under its yoke [and refused to work]! The gentile beat the cow, but still it would not budge. Seeing this, the gentile went to the Jew and said, "Come and take back your cow! Is it perhaps ill? — for though I beat it, it refuses to budge!"*
>
> *The Jew understood that it was because of Shabbos that the animal did not work, for it was accustomed to resting on Shabbos [as the halachah requires]. The Jew said, "Come and I will cause the cow to stand up and work." He went and whispered in the cow's ear, "You know that when you were mine, you worked for six days and rested on Shabbos. Now that due to my sins you are under the domain of a gentile, I ask of you that you stand up and work." Immediately, the cow arose and began to work.*
>
> *The gentile said, ". . .I will not let you go until you tell me what you whispered, for I became weary from beating it and still it would not stand up!" The Jew replied, "I used no sorcery. Rather, I whispered such and such in her ear, and she plowed."*
>
> *The gentile was awestruck. He said: "If a cow that has no power of speech and no intellect recognized her Creator, then I, who was created in His image and was endowed with intellect, should certainly recognize Him!" He immediately went and converted, studied, and merited [to absorb the teachings of] Torah. They called him Yochanan ben Torta*

[Yochanan the product of the cow]. Until this day, our Sages relate certain laws in his name.

The Torah states: וּבַיּוֹם הַשְּׁבִיעִי תִּשְׁבֹּת לְמַעַן יָנוּחַ שׁוֹרְךָ וַחֲמֹרֶךָ, *And on the seventh day you shall rest, so that your ox and donkey may rest (Exodus 23:12).* What is the significance of the term לְמַעַן, *so that?*

Imrei Emes explains: You shall experience the Shabbos in such a manner that the aura of your observance will be felt by your surroundings — including your livestock, as in the case of Yochanan ben Torta.[1]

For All Generations

And the Children of Israel shall keep the Shabbos, to make the Shabbos an eternal covenant for their generations (Exodus 31:16).

◦§ There is a misconception among some that Shabbos was intended as a day of rest from the physical work of the previous six days. This cannot possibly be true, for Shabbos was given to the Jews in the Wilderness, where their needs were provided through miracles and they engaged in no physical labor at all! To them, Shabbos could only be a day of spiritual striving — and the same holds true *for their generations (K'sav Sofer).*

Let no one think that the sanctity of the day could be perceived

---

1. In his *Divrei Yechezkel*, R' Yechezkel of Shiniv relates that a *ger*, convert, once complained of the following: In the Ten Commandments, the Torah states, *But the seventh day is the Shabbos for* HASHEM, *your God; you may do no work — you, your son and your daughter, your slave and your maidservant, your animal, and the convert that is in your gates.* In this verse, animals are mentioned before the convert. Doesn't this insinuate that Judaism places its livestock ahead of its converts?

R' Yechezkel countered with a simple response. The Torah groups together all those whose abstention from labor is the responsibility of the adult Jew mentioned first in the verse. One must not permit his children, slaves, or even his livestock to work. However, nowhere are we commanded to ensure that a convert observe Shabbos, for a convert is responsible for himself as is any other independent Jew. This is why the convert is placed last in the verse.

Michtam L'David offers another response to the convert's question. The Torah places livestock ahead of the convert to teach that if a Jew observes Shabbos properly, then the aura of Shabbos will be felt by even his animals, who in turn, may be the cause of a gentile becoming a convert — as in the case of Yochanan ben Torta.

only by the *tzaddikim* of earlier generations. Rather, in *all generations* — even in our lowly era — a Jew can merit to perceive the day's loftiness if he will but properly prepare himself for it (*Divrei Emunah*).

The way in which one experiences the Shabbos is usually reflected in the Shabbos observance of his offspring. If one truly delights in the Shabbos, utilizing it as a day of spiritual growth, then his children will do the same. However, if one views Shabbos as nothing more than a restful day of work abstention, devoid of any positive meaning, then his children may, God forbid, not even live up to his minimal observance. Thus does the Torah state: *And the Children of Israel shall keep the Shabbos* — in such a way that the Shabbos will remain an eternal covenant for all generations.[1]

Awaiting the Queen

He who expends effort prior to the Shabbos shall eat on the Shabbos (Avodah Zarah 3a).

Light's Reflection

◆§ Just as the spiritual reward of the World to Come is commensurate with one's preparation in this world, so it is with the Shabbos. How one merits to perceive the Shabbos depends largely on his spiritual

---

1. In a well-known address, R' Moshe Feinstein traced the decline of religious observance among American Jewish immigrants in the early part of this century to their parents' attitude regarding Shabbos. Shabbos observance was a great test of faith at that time, since many employers would not permit workers a day off on Saturday. The average Shabbos observer struggled hard, as he floated from job to job in search of the peace and prosperity that he hoped to find in the *'Golde'ne Medinah'* ('Golden Land'). The attitudes of the immigrants in their struggles varied. Some rose to the challenge, accepting their hardships with unquestioning faith — and even exhilaration over their self-sacrifice. Others, however, would come home and — in front of their children — lament as *s'iz shver tzu zein a Yid* (that it is difficult being a Jew). When these children grew up and were on their own, they saw no reason to endure their parents' hardships, of which they had no understanding. Thus, they forsook their parents' observant ways.

performance during the previous six days. R' Shmel'ke of Nikolsburg (*Divrei Shmuel*) found an analogy for this in the reflection of
sunlight on a wall. The light will appear to be whatever color the
wall is. The spiritual radiance of Shabbos is reflected in each soul in
accordance with what that soul has achieved in the week that has
passed.

From Joy to Mourning

∽§ In *Lamentations* (5:15), we read: שָׁבַת מְשׂוֹשׂ לִבֵּנוּ נֶהְפַּךְ לְאֵבֶל מְחוֹלֵנוּ,
Gone is the joy of our hearts, our dancing has turned into mourning.
R' Menachem Mendel of Rimanov explained this homiletically: שַׁבָּת
מְשׂוֹשׂ לִבֵּנוּ — Shabbos which should be the joy of our hearts, נֶהְפַּךְ
לְאֵבֶל — has turned into a day of mourning, for instead of savoring
every moment of this day, some wait for the moment when they can
recite *havdalah* and return to their mundane activities. What is the
source of this attitude? מְחוֹלֵנוּ — It is because of our weekdays (חול),
i.e., the manner in which the weekdays that precede the Shabbos
are spent.

Waiting and Anticipating

וְשָׁמְרוּ בְנֵי יִשְׂרָאֵל אֶת הַשַּׁבָּת.
And the Children of Israel shall keep the Shabbos (*Exodus*
31:16).

∽§ The previous verses reiterate the command to observe the Shabbos
which had already been stated in the Ten Commandments. It follows, then, that the exhortation here to 'keep the Shabbos' means
something more than mere observance. *Ohr HaChaim* interprets
these words in a number of ways. Two of his interpretations follow:

1) The word וְשָׁמְרוּ, commonly translated *and they shall keep*, also
connotes *watchful anticipation* as in וְאָבִיו שָׁמַר אֶת הַדָּבָר, *but his
father kept the matter in mind* (*Genesis* 37:11; see *Rashi*). Rather
than see Shabbos as a burden and a day of restriction, a Jew should
learn to appreciate Shabbos for the day of blessing that it is. And this
appreciation should manifest itself each week in one's eager
anticipation of the approaching Shabbos.

2) One should await the Shabbos by being מוֹסִיף מֵחוֹל עַל הַקּוֹדֶשׁ, that
is, to accept the day's sanctity upon oneself and refrain from all

forbidden activities even before the setting of the sun, when Shabbos would otherwise begin (see *Orach Chaim* 261:2). By doing this, one is in effect readying himself to greet the Shabbos Queen in the way of a groom who, at the *chuppah* ceremony, goes forth to meet his beloved bride (see p. 73).

The Satmar *Rav (Divrei Yoel)* explained that there is a degree of anticipation at the close of Shabbos as well. In the *Hoshanos* prayer recited on the Shabbos of Succos, we say: הוֹשַׁע נָא] יוֹשֶׁבֶת וּמַמְתֶּנֶת עַד כְּלוֹת שַׁבָּת, *[Please save the People that] sits and waits until the end of Shabbos*. The apparent meaning of these words implies praise of those who sit staring at their watches until the moment that Shabbos ends! In fact, the waiting mentioned here means the very opposite. Shabbos observance is, of course, explicitly stated in the Torah. However, *tosafos Shabbos*, adding to the Shabbos both at its beginning and conclusion, is derived by the Sages through Scriptural exegesis (see *Yoma* 81b). In commenting on a verse in *Song of Songs* (1:2), the Talmud relates that the Jewish Nation said to the Holy One: עֲרֵבִים עָלַי דִּבְרֵי דּוֹדֶיךָ יוֹתֵר מִיֵּינָהּ שֶׁל תּוֹרָה, *The words of Your beloved ones [i.e., the Sages] are more pleasant to me than the wine of Torah*, meaning that the expositions of the Sages — without which the Written Law is incomplete and often not understandable — are more precious than the Written Law itself.

As Shabbos draws to a close, the Jewish People wait for the moment when their observance of the day is in the category of *tosafos Shabbos*, as the Sages taught. Once that moment arrives, they extend the Shabbos yet longer, savoring each moment of this most coveted of days.

Cause and Effect

כִּי שֵׁשֶׁת יָמִים עָשָׂה ה' אֶת הַשָּׁמַיִם וְאֶת הָאָרֶץ. . .
For in six days Hashem made heaven and earth. . . (Exodus 31:17).

◆§ The wording of this verse is difficult, for its plain meaning should have required the word בְּשֵׁשֶׁת, *[for] in six [days Hashem created. . .]*, rather than שֵׁשֶׁת, *six*. In a homiletic sense, כִּי שֵׁשֶׁת יָמִים עָשָׂה ה' can be interpreted, *for Hashem created six days*. Each week is a creation for itself, a product of the Shabbos observance that immediately precedes it. Just as the continued existence of the universe is contingent on the study of Torah (*Pesachim* 68b), so is it contingent on the keeping of Shabbos. Were there not at least some Jews keeping any given Shabbos, the world would return to nothingness (*Ohr HaChaim*).

Thus does *Zohar* teach that all Heavenly wrathful decrees and grievances are silenced in Heaven with the onset of Shabbos. Shabbos signals a new beginning, a fresh start for all of creation (*Bnei Yissochor*). It is for man to seize the moment, and make the most of this day of renewal. If he observes the Shabbos properly, then it is he who has caused the next six days to be. How illuminating, then, is the Talmudic teaching (*Shabbos* 119b) that upon reciting the chapter of וַיְכֻלּוּ הַשָּׁמַיִם at the onset of Shabbos, one has become a partner with Hashem in the creation of the world![1]

Remember the Shabbos Day

זָכוֹר אֶת יוֹם הַשַּׁבָּת לְקַדְּשׁוֹ.

Remember the Shabbos day to sanctify it (The Ten Commandments, Exodus 20:8).

◦§ *Mechilta* derives from the word זָכוֹר, *Remember*, that the Shabbos should be in one's thoughts throughout the week. "R' Yitzchak says, 'Do not count days as others count them, rather you should count every weekday in relation to the Shabbos.' " *Ramban* elaborates: Other nations consider the days of the week to be unrelated to one another. This is why they call the days by separate names, each after a different Heavenly force [i.e., Sunday after the sun, Monday after the moon, etc.]. Israel, however, counts all days in reference to the Shabbos, as we preface the *Song of the Day* at the conclusion of *Shacharis*, "Today is the first day of the Shabbos. . ." "Today is the second day. . ." Through constant remembrance of the Shabbos, one will forever be cognizant of the existence of God, Who created the world in six days and commanded us to rest on the seventh.

Moreover, our remembrance should be one of לְקַדְּשׁוֹ, *to sanctify it*: "[One should bear in mind] that the cessation of work [on this day] is because it is a hallowed day, a day on which to turn away from our preoccupations with the vanities of life, and grant delight to our souls by following God's path and hearing His word from the mouths of sages and prophets, as it is written: '*Why do you go to him [i.e., the prophet] today? — it is not Rosh Chodesh or Shabbos!*' (*II Kings* 4:23) — for such was their way" (*Ramban*, ibid.).

---

1. See p. 43.

Remember. . .to Sanctify

⋙ Since the purpose of 'Remember' is 'to sanctify it,' one must prepare himself throughout the week in order to be a proper receptacle for the sanctity of Shabbos. It is through proper preparation that one absorbs the day's blessings (Nesivos Shalom).

"Remember the Shabbos day to sanctify it — Establish the Shabbos as an eternal pillar of knowledge of God and His sanctity! In order to demonstrate this concept, you must restrain your power of dominion in this world on the day of Shabbos. On this day, you must return the world that was entrusted to you, so that you will always realize in your heart that this world is loaned to you but temporarily.

"Do you not realize that Shabbos is entirely a sign, remembrance and covenant?! Rather than a day of rest from the toil of the past week, the Shabbos proclaims sanctity, as the source of spirituality and sanctity for the days of toil that follow" (R' Samson Raphael Hirsch).

Hillel and Shammai

⋙ In explaining the command 'Remember,' Rashi cites the way of Shammai the Elder who 'remembered' the Shabbos throughout the week by preparing for it as soon as the previous Shabbos had ended.

> They said of Shammai the Elder that all his days he ate in honor of Shabbos. When he came across a beautiful animal, he would say, "This will be for Shabbos." If he came across a nicer one, he would set aside the second one and consume the first during the weekdays.
>
> However, Hillel the Elder had a different approach, for all his deeds were for the sake of Heaven, as it is written, "Blessed is my Lord for every single day" (Beitzah 16a).

As Rashi (ibid.) explains, Hillel was confident that, as Shabbos approached, Heaven would provide him with what he needed in order to honor the day. Therefore, he did not set aside food from the beginning of the week.

Mishnah Berurah (250:3), citing the opinion of many earlier commentators, writes that even Hillel would agree that the way of

Shammai is preferable for most people. Hillel, however, possessed an unusual degree of trust in the One Above. In order to further strengthen that trust, he would wait for God to send his Shabbos needs later in the week, rather than set things aside at the week's beginning.[1]

The Shabbos Experience

The Thirty-Nine Forbidden Labors

◆§ After God instructed Moses to construct the *Mishkan* (Tabernacle), He repeated the commandment of the Shabbos (*Exodus* 31:12-17). In imparting to the nation the command to build the *Mishkan*, Moses first commanded them again regarding the Shabbos (ibid. 35:1-3). From this our Sages derive that: 1) The construction of the *Mishkan* did not supersede the Shabbos (*Shabbos* 70a). 2) Every form of labor that was needed in the *Mishkan*'s construction is forbidden on Shabbos (ibid. 49b).

Why did God choose the *Mishkan* as the vehicle through which the Shabbos laws are derived?

The *Mishkan*'s construction was led by Bezalel, who was imbued with Heavenly knowledge, wisdom and understanding (*Exodus* 31:3). Our Sages (*Berachos* 55a) teach:

יוֹדֵעַ הָיָה בְּצַלְאֵל לְצָרֵף אוֹתִיּוֹת שֶׁנִּבְרְאוּ בָהֶם שָׁמַיִם וָאָרֶץ.
Bezalel knew how to combine the letters with which heaven and earth were created.

The *Mishkan* was a microcosm of all creation (*Tanchuma, Pikudei* 2). Indeed, many commentators explain how each part of the structure and service in the *Mishkan* symbolized an aspect of the physical world. The construction of the *Mishkan* represented man's responsibility to elevate and sanctify all of creation toward the service of its Creator. Through such service, man becomes a partner with God, as it were, in bringing the world toward its ultimate goal and perfection — and he causes the *Shechinah* (Divine Presence) to dwell on this earth.

---

1. *Mishnah Berurah* adds that even Hillel would set aside a rare item that was not likely to be available later in the week.

Just as the *Mishkan* was a microcosm of creation, so was each aspect of its construction a parallel to an aspect of God's creation. This is why to qualify as builder of the *Mishkan*, Bezalel had to be proficient in utilizing the spiritual forces through which heaven and earth were created. The cessation of the construction on Shabbos was an exact parallel of God's cessation of work on the seventh day of creation. This is why the Shabbos laws are derived from the *Mishkan*.

Like Dew

◄§ As the *Mishnah* (*Shabbos* 7:2) states, all forbidden labors on Shabbos are categorized under one or more of the ל״ט אֲבוֹת מְלָאכוֹת, *thirty-nine primary labors* that were performed in constructing the *Mishkan*. The letters ל and ט (39) form the word טַל, *dew*. Initially, keeping the laws of Shabbos may seem difficult and even burdensome. It is a Jew's obligation, however, to develop an appreciation for the loftiness and beauty of Shabbos, to the point that its observance will be as pleasant as the gentle falling of dew. Then, he will merit the day's infinite blessings (*Ben Yehoyada*).

Remember and Safeguard

שָׁמוֹר אֶת יוֹם הַשַּׁבָּת לְקַדְּשׁוֹ.
Safeguard the Shabbos day to sanctify it (The Ten Commandments, Deuteronomy 5:12).

◄§ Whereas in the first version of the Ten Commandments the commandment of Shabbos opens with the word זָכוֹר, *Remember*, in the second version it opens with שָׁמוֹר, *Safeguard*. *Remember* is a positive commandment to "remember" the day both in our thoughts and through verbal expression (see pp. 52,80). *Safeguard* is a negative commandment which warns us to prevent and refrain from desecrating the Shabbos.

With reference to these variant texts, the Sages (*Mechilta, Shavuos* 20b) taught: "זָכוֹר, *Remember*, and שָׁמוֹר, *Safeguard,* were both said in a single utterance." This superhuman feat was performed by God when He gave this commandment, its purpose being to demonstrate to Israel that the positive and negative aspects of Shabbos observance are interrelated. In the words of *R' Samson Raphael Hirsch:*

"This intimate connection between the concepts of שָׁמוֹר and זָכוֹר, the physical demonstration and the spiritual adoption of one and the same truth. . . clearly reveals to us the requirement that is basic to all of our vocation as Jews. . . The spurious concept of a so-called 'adoration of God in spirit and truth' — in which the spirit is supposed to soar heavenward while the body is free to wallow far away from God in the cesspool of animal lust — should be foreign to Judaism."

Rich and Poor Alike

•§ The rich find the charge of זָכוֹר much easier than that of שָׁמוֹר. They have little difficulty enhancing the Shabbos with meat, wine and other delights. They may, however, find it difficult to totally abstain from any work-related act, instruction or discussion, all of which fall under the command to protect the day's sanctity in a negative sense.

The very opposite is true of the poor. They have little problem refraining from business matters since they have not much to discuss. However, to apportion of their limited funds for the festive Shabbos meals may for them be a test of faith, not to mention physical strain. God therefore uttered זָכוֹר and שָׁמוֹר simultaneously, to show that one should not be neglectful in fulfilling either of these commands (*Dubno Maggid*).

'HASHEM Is One'

•§ Rashi (*Exodus* 20:1 citing *Mechilta*) states that at the giving of the Ten Commandments, the Jews responded "Yes" after each positive commandment and "No" after each negative commandment. Now, if by the *mitzvah* of Shabbos, the positive זָכוֹר and negative שָׁמוֹר were uttered simultaneously, how did the Jews respond? The answer is found in the *'Yom Shabboson'* song of Shabbos day: וּפָתְחוּ וְעָנוּ ה׳ אֶחָד, *They opened their mouths and called out "HASHEM is One!"* — for the total Shabbos experience is a declaration of faith in the One and Only God (*R' Avraham Mordechai of Ger*).

'Then You Shall Be Granted Pleasure'

אִם תָּשִׁיב מִשַּׁבָּת רַגְלֶךָ עֲשׂוֹת חֲפָצֶךָ בְּיוֹם קָדְשִׁי וְקָרָאתָ לַשַּׁבָּת עֹנֶג לִקְדוֹשׁ ה׳ מְכֻבָּד וְכִבַּדְתּוֹ מֵעֲשׂוֹת דְּרָכֶיךָ מִמְּצוֹא חֶפְצְךָ וְדַבֵּר דָּבָר. אָז תִּתְעַנַּג עַל ה׳ וְהִרְכַּבְתִּיךָ עַל בָּמֳתֵי אָרֶץ וְהַאֲכַלְתִּיךָ נַחֲלַת יַעֲקֹב אָבִיךָ כִּי פִּי ה׳ דִּבֵּר.

If you restrain, because of the Shabbos, your feet, refrain from attending to your mundane needs on My holy day; if you proclaim the Shabbos, 'a delight,' the holy one of HASHEM, 'honored one,' and you honor it by not doing your own ways, from seeking your personal mundane needs or discussing the forbidden. Then you shall be granted pleasure with HASHEM and I shall mount you astride the heights of the world, and I shall provide you with the heritage of your father Jacob — for the mouth of HASHEM has spoken (Isaiah 58:13-14)

◄§ Rambam (*Hilchos Shabbos* 30:1) writes: "Four things were said regarding the Shabbos, two are ordained by the Torah while the other two were derived by the Sages from the words of the Prophets. Those from the Torah are derived from זָכוֹר and שָׁמוֹר, *Remember* and *Safeguard. Kavod* and *Oneg*, honor and delight, were taught by the Prophets, as it is written: וְקָרָאתָ לַשַּׁבָּת עֹנֶג לִקְדוֹשׁ ה׳ מְכֻבָּד, *if you proclaim the Shabbos 'a delight,' the holy one of HASHEM, 'honored one.'*"

Kavod

◄§ "What did the Sages mean by כָּבוֹד, *honor?* It is a *mitzvah* for a person to wash his face, hands and feet with warm water on *Erev Shabbos* in honor of Shabbos, then to wrap himself in a garment of *tzitzis* and sit with awe as he waits to greet the Shabbos — as if he would be going out to greet a king. The early Sages would gather their disciples on *erev Shabbos*, wrap themselves and say, 'Come, let us go out to greet the Shabbos king.'[1]

"Also included in *kavod*, honor, is that one should don clean clothing and that his Shabbos garments should not be ones which he wears during the weekdays" (*ibid.* §2-3).

In his preface to *Zichru Toras Moshe*, R' Avraham Danzig (author of *Chayei Adam*) writes:

"As the sanctity of this day is exceedingly great, it is the Holy One's desire that we earn merit through our acquiring an additional soul[2] and absorbing the day's sanctity. Therefore, He commanded us

---

1. According to our Talmudic texts, the Sages referred to Shabbos as מַלְכָּה, *Queen.*

2. Earlier, R' Danzig writes: "One can understand and test that when he will focus his thoughts properly and when the awe of God will truly fill his heart so that his deeds be pleasing [to God], then surely after he will immerse himself [in a *mikveh*] with proper intent to accept upon himself the sanctity of Shabbos, he will himself perceive the additional soul within him."

to honor this day and delight in it to the point that — as our Sages state — Shabbos observance is equivalent to [observance of] the entire Torah and its desecration is akin to idol-worship. We are therefore obligated to honor the Shabbos in every way possible. . . Let everyone imagine that a king has come to his home — for even greater than this is the holy Shabbos, through which one acquires a portion of a hallowed soul, which is called a *lamp of God* (*Proverbs* 20:27).

"Praiseworthy are those who perceive the meaning of בּוֹאִי כַלָּה, *'Enter, O Bride!'* Surely, they will become gripped by awe and trepidation, and will honor this Bride more than they would a king of flesh and blood."

Shabbos Preparations

◄§ The *Halachah* places great importance on the actual preparations for the Shabbos, which fall under the category of *kavod*, honor for the day. *Shulchan Aruch* (*Orach Chaim* 250:1) states:

"One should rise early on Friday to prepare that which is needed for Shabbos. Even if one has many servants to serve him, he should strive to prepare [at least] something himself for the Shabbos, in order to give the day honor. As we find regarding [the Talmudic sages]: R' Chisda would thinly slice vegtables; Rabbah and R' Yosef would chop wood; R' Zeira would kindle a fire; and R' Nachman would prepare the house by bringing the Shabbos vessels in and taking the weekday vessels out. All should take a lesson from these Sages and not say, 'Such is beneath my dignity,' for through this — giving honor to the Shabbos — one is honored."

A number of comments by the Chofetz Chaim to the above are particularly noteworthy:

□ *One should rise early on Friday* — It is preferable to prepare for Shabbos on Friday rather than on Thursday, for in this way, it is more obvious that the preparations are, indeed, for Shabbos. Obviously, foods that require long preparation [i.e., pickling] should be done on Thursday. In the winter, when Fridays are short, much of the preparing should be done on Thursday (*Mishnah Berurah* §2).

□ *Even if one has many servants* — For the *mitzvah* to honor the Shabbos is incumbent on everyone, as it is written: "If you proclaim the Shabbos 'a delight', the holy one of HASHEM, 'honored one.'" As with regard to all *mitzvos*, "The *mitzvah* is better executed through him rather than through his designate" [*Kiddushin* 41a] (*Mishnah Berurah* §3).

□ *He should strive to prepare* — In codifying this *halachah*, *Rambam* (*Hilchos Shabbos* 30:6) writes: "Even one who is highly prominent and is unaccustomed to shopping in the market or involving himself with domestic chores is nonetheless obligated to physically perform tasks for the sake of the Shabbos — for this is his honor." *Rambam*'s use of the term חַיָּב, *one is obligated*, implies that it is a halachic obligation to physically take part in the Shabbos preparations. However, from the fact that the Talmud only uses this term regarding the honoring of the day through candle-lighting, it would seem that other aspects of *kavod Shabbos* do not carry this same stringency. *Rambam* would then mean that to physically prepare for Shabbos is *similar* to an obligation (כעין חובה), for if not, these Talmudic Sages would not have interrupted their study of Torah for it (*Beur Halachah*, s.v.ישתדל).

□ *For through this one is honored* — *Responsa Chavos Yair* wonders how these Sages permitted themselves to perform chores that seem beneath their dignity, for we know that the Torah attaches great importance to human dignity (see *Berachos* 19b). The answer to this is found in these words of *Shulchan Aruch*: *for through this he is honored*. In performing these tasks, the Sages were fulfilling a *mitzvah*, and it was obvious that what they were doing was for the honor of the One Above. Similarly, we find that David did that which seemed beneath his dignity as King of Israel, for the sake of God and His Torah (*Beur Halachah*, s.v. כי זהו כבודו).

Oneg

◦§ *Rambam* further states:

"What is עֹנֶג, *delight*? It is that which the Sages said, to prepare for Shabbos a dish that is exceptionally rich and a drink that is especially refreshing — each man according to his means. Whoever is generous with his expenditures for the Shabbos, and in preparing many good foods for it, is praiseworthy. However, if he cannot afford much, then even if he cooks a single stew or something similar in honor of Shabbos, this too is *oneg* Shabbos" (§7).

Body and Soul

~§ R' Yisrael Ba'al Shem Tov explained the mitzvah of oneg with a parable:

A prince was taken captive and was brought to a place far away from home, where the people were ignorant and accorded him no respect. One day, the prince received a letter from home. He was overjoyed and wanted desperately to express his feelings. He felt like jumping up and dancing, but how could he when everyone around him would laugh and taunt him? Then, he had an idea. He purchased some food and some good wine and invited his neighbors to a feast. They gorged themselves and became drunk until they began to sing and dance. The prince, too, danced, but for a different reason. The neighbors danced out of drunkenness; he danced from exultation over the letter he had received.

Similarly, said the Ba'al Shem Tov, the soul yearns to exult over the heightened spiritual state that it experiences on Shabbos. However, the physical body in which the soul resides does not feel this same exultation and it inhibits the soul's delight. Therefore, we give the body what it desires — good food and drink — so that it will gain satisfaction from the day and allow the soul to delight in its spiritual pleasure.

The above is complemented by another parable of the Ba'al Shem Tov:

Once there was a king who announced that for one day, each of his many subjects could come forth and be granted a request. One of his subjects was a man who suffered from a severe, chronic skin disease. He asked the king, "Please, Your Majesty, provide me with an ample supply of earth, which when applied, provides me temporary relief from my ailment. Also, I find it soothing to rub my skin against brick and stone from time to time. However, the police do not allow me this relief, for they say that it is improper to do such things in public. Please make an exception for me."

Those who heard the man's request laughed incredulously. "How foolish of you!" they cried. "Instead of asking for that which gives you temporary relief, you should have asked that the king spare no cost to provide you the best doctors and medications so that you can be permanently cured."

Said the Ba'al Shem Tov: The mitzvah of oneg Shabbos is a means through which one can derive fully the great spiritual blessings of the day. How pitiful it is when the eating and drinking become an end unto themselves (*Otzar Mishlei Chassidim*).

A Higher Level

⋖§ Physical pleasure in this world can be a highly spiritual experience. This is especially true regarding a *mitzvah* as fundamental as Shabbos. Note the following from *Michtav Me'Eliyahu* (Vol. III, p. 226):

"There are many *mitzvos* in the Torah whose goal is to sanctify the physical by using it to fulfill God's command. . .The main focus of such commandments is that man's primary striving be the *mitzvah* itself and the pleasure derived thereby be only secondary — for example, the concept of *oneg Shabbos*, the intent of which is that one *bring delight to the Shabbos*, meaning that through the eating of tasty foods and the wearing of fine clothing, one develop within himself an appreciation for the exalted status of Shabbos.

"However, the *yetzer hara*, evil inclination, is extremely cunning with regard to such *mitzvos*. He induces man to seek only physical pleasure and he conceals this sinful attitude in the guise of a *mitzvah* which requires one to experience that pleasure. The result is that *kedushah*, sanctity, is transformed into *tumah*, impurity. . .It is with regard to this that R' Yisrael Salanter said: *"Men est dach oif dem Shabbos in tzimmis"* (The entire Shabbos is consumed [i.e., destroyed] with the delicacies!)

Whoever Brings Delight

Whoever brings delight to the Shabbos is granted an inheritance without constrictions. . .is saved from servitude to the gentile kingdoms. . . is granted his heart's desires (Shabbos 118a-b).

Shelah notes that the above reads כָּל הַמְעַנֵּג אֶת הַשַּׁבָּת, *Whoever brings delight to the Shabbos*, rather than כָּל הַמְעַנֵּג בְּשַׁבָּת, *Whoever delights on the Shabbos*. One should ensure that *oneg Shabbos* is done for the sake of the Shabbos, rather than for his own sake.

Shelah continues: ". . .One should use proper judgment and exercise foresight when he sits down to eat, so that his being satiated will not prevent him from remaining awake to toil in Torah and *mitzvos*. Rather, he should eat and drink with joy and a happy heart, good foods that are tasty and easily digested — modest in quantity but great in quality. Then he should arise from his joyous meal to begin his fixed session of Torah study."

Measure for Measure

◦§ The commentators explain how the rewards for *oneg Shabbos* mentioned above are commensurate with the *mitzvah*:

The *mitzvah* of *tosafos Shabbos*, adding to the Shabbos (see p. 50), is one that has no limit. One can extend the Shabbos as long into the night as he pleases. Those who truly delight in the Shabbos will often extend the Shabbos past the required time. In the merit of not limiting their *oneg Shabbos*, they will be rewarded with *an inheritance without constrictions* (*Ben Yehoyada*).

While proper Shabbos observance is a truly delightful experience, it can sometimes involve personal hardship and sacrifice. For example, one who is unexpectedly forced to spend Shabbos on the road may encounter great difficulties. Nevertheless, a devout Jew will not compromise his Shabbos observance even under such conditions. Accepting upon oneself to observe Shabbos in all circumstances is a form of *kabalas ol malchus shamayim*, acceptance of the yoke of the Kingdom of Heaven. In this merit, *one is saved from servitude to gentile kingdoms* (*Eitz Yosef* citing *Levush*).

According to the strict dictates of *Halachah*, discussion of one's mundane activities is forbidden on Shabbos (*Orach Chaim* ch.307), but it is permissible to ponder them in one's mind. However, those who truly delight in the Shabbos will drive all such thoughts from their minds on this day. In the merit of opening their minds and hearts completely to the blessings of Shabbos, they will be *granted their hearts' desires* (*Ben Yehoyada*).

A Sign for All Mitzvos

אַךְ אֶת שַׁבְּתֹתַי תִּשְׁמֹרוּ כִּי אוֹת הִיא בֵּינִי וּבֵינֵיכֶם לְדֹרֹתֵיכֶם לָדַעַת כִּי אֲנִי ה' מְקַדִּשְׁכֶם.

But My Shabbos you are to safeguard, for it is a sign between Me and you for your generations, to know that I am HASHEM Who sanctifies you (Exodus 31:13).

◦§ The *Dubno Maggid* explained the above verse with a parable:

A wealthy man purchased expensive material from which a

beautiful set of clothing would be sewn for his son. The material was given to a tailor who was instructed to present each garment to the son as soon as it was finished.

When the son had received all but one piece of his new outfit, he donned them and proudly went out into the street. As he walked, he encountered a young ruffian who eyed the handsome clothing jealously. The ruffian could not bear to see the rich boy dressed so well, so he grabbed him, tore his clothing and threw him into the mud. The garments would never be the same.

Later, when the tailor finished the last piece of clothing, the father told his son, "Please take care of this garment, for it is the only one whose original beauty is still intact. Let it always be a reminder to you of the beautiful set of clothing that I had once given you."

Explained the *Dubno Maggid:* Physical activities such as eating and drinking are acts of instant pleasure. *Mitzvah* performance, however, is something that provides pleasure not instantly, but as a reward in the World to Come. In fact, this was not the situation prior to Adam's partaking of the Tree of Knowledge. Before that sin, performing a *mitzvah* was an act of instant, immeasurable spiritual pleasure. At the time of the Final Redemption, the world will revert back to its original state, and performing a *mitzvah* will once again provide us with a kind of immediate pleasure to which no physical gratification can compare.

Only one *mitzvah* was untouched by Adam's sin. Because Adam sinned on the sixth day of creation, the Shabbos — which had not yet come into being — was unaffected. Thus, even today, the Shabbos can still be experienced in the way that was originally intended. Indeed, the restful contentment of the day, coupled with the festive eating and drinking that is a very integral part of the Shabbos experience, make it relatively easy for virtually anyone to feel pleasure from this *mitzvah*.

Thus did God instruct His People: *"But My Shabbos you are to safeguard"*: Ensure that your Shabbos observance be wholesome and beautiful; do not taint it in any way. *". . .for it is a sign between Me and you for their generations"* — It is a sign for all generations of the immediate, infinite pleasure that one could have derived from all *mitzvos* as was originally intended. *"..to know that I am HASHEM Who sanctifies you"* — in Messianic times, when every *mitzvah* will be experienced as is the Shabbos today.[1]

1. See *Yalkut Shimoni* to *Exodus* 31:13.

Guaranteed Returns

The Holy One told the Jewish People: "My son, borrow for My sake and sanctify the day. Have faith in Me and I will pay back."

. . . A person's entire sustenance [for the coming year] is fixed between Rosh Hashanah and Yom Kippur with the exception of his expenses for Shabbos and Yom Tov, and his expenses for having his sons study Torah. [With regard to these expenses,] if he is frugal, he will be granted less and if he is generous, he will be granted more (Beitzah 15b-16a).

◄§ In connection with the above, the Talmud (see *Tosafos* ibid.) cites the following verse: *Go eat rich foods and drink sweet drinks, send portions to one who has none prepared, for the day is sanctified unto our Master; do not be upset, for rejoicing for the sake of God is your strength (Nechemiah* 8:10). *Rashi* explains the last phrase to mean that the joy with which one honors the Shabbos will gain him the necessary merit so that his expenditures for Shabbos needs will be replenished.

As Best as We Can

◄§ The passage of *Bircas Kohanim*, the Priestly Blessing (*Numbers* 6:22-27), opens with God instructing Moses to command the Kohanim: כֹּה תְבָרְכוּ אֶת בְּנֵי יִשְׂרָאֵל אָמוֹר לָהֶם, *So shall you bless the Children of Israel, saying to them.* Regarding the word אָמוֹר, *saying, Rashi* comments: אָמוֹר כְּמוֹ זָכוֹר וְשָׁמוֹר, *[The structure of the word]* אָמוֹר *is analogous to that of* זָכוֹר *(Remember the Shabbos) and* שָׁמוֹר *(Safeguard the Shabbos).*

R' Tzvi Hirsh of Rimanov explained this comment of *Rashi* homiletically, based on the following story:

In his younger years, R' Tzvi Hirsh served as an attendant in the house of his predecessor, R' Menacham Mendel of Rimanov. One Thursday, there was not a cent in the house with which to purchase food for Shabbos. R' Menachem Mendel's *rebbetzin* sent R' Tzvi Hirsh to ask her husband what to do. Before R' Tzvi Hirsh could say anything, R' Menachem Mendel said, "Take the pot in which the fish is usually cooked, fill it with the usual amount of water and place it on the fire. Do the same with the meat pot, as well as with the other pots in which the Shabbos foods are cooked."

"But, *Rebbe*," R' Tzvi Hirsh protested, "what will we put in the pots? We have neither food nor money with which to purchase anything!"

The *tzaddik* then explained: "Regarding the manna which fell in the Wilderness, the Jews were commanded: *And on the sixth day [i.e. Erev Shabbos] they shall prepare that which they shall bring in (Exodus* 16:5). It is for us to make the preparations to the best of our abilities. The Holy Day itself will bring whatever else we need."

No sooner had the pots been put on the stove than a stranger appeared at the door. He had been passing through the town and had decided to spend Shabbos there. He asked if he could lodge at the *Rebbe*'s house, while adding that he was not in need of food, for he always carried with him a supply of food for Shabbos. In fact, he had brought so much food along that he was able to treat his hosts to very sumptuous Shabbos meals.

R' Tzvi Hirsh explained: *Rashi* is comparing the blessing of the *Kohanim* to the *mitzvah* of Shabbos in the following way: It is obvious that the *Kohanim* are not the ultimate source of the blessings that they confer. The *Kohanim* can do nothing more than make the proper preparations — wash their hands, lift them upwards and chant the appropriate verses with proper concentration. Then God Himself comes and grants the fulfillment of וַאֲנִי אֲבָרֲכֵם, *And I shall bless them (Numbers* 6:27).

And so it is with Shabbos. It is for us to prepare for Shabbos as best as we can; the rest we leave to God.

Yosef Mokir Shabbos

◆§ The Talmud (*Shabbos* 119a) cites the well-known story of 'Yosef *Mokir [who honors] Shabbos*':

There was a man named Yosef who was well known for the manner in which he honored the Shabbos. In Yosef's neighborhood there lived a very wealthy gentile. One day, astrologers told the gentile, "All your wealth is destined to become that of Yosef *Mokir Shabbos*." In order to thwart their prediction, the gentile went and sold his entire estate. With the sale money, he purchased a single pearl which was then placed into a gold setting on a hat which he wore.

One day as the gentile was crossing a bridge, a gust of wind blew the hat off his head. The hat fell into the water below and was swallowed by a large fish. The fish was caught and brought to the market late Friday afternoon. The fishermen asked, "Who will buy such a fish at this late hour?" "Bring it to Yosef *Mokir Shabbos*," they were told, "for he is in the habit of making such purchases." They brought the fish to Yosef and he bought it. When he cut open the fish, he found the hat with the pearl. Yosef sold the pearl for the huge fortune that it was worth. At that time, a סָבָא, *elder*, met Yosef and remarked, "One who borrows for the Shabbos [i.e., who goes to great expense for its sake], the Shabbos pays back."

Iyun Yaakov explains that Yosef *Mokir Shabbos* was accustomed to spending far above his means to honor the Shabbos, and this made him the object of the gentile's ridicule. It was therefore decreed in Heaven that the gentile would be punished by losing his entire fortune and that Yosef would be rewarded for his efforts by acquiring the gentile's wealth.

As *Anaf Yosef* notes, the way through which the gentile hoped to retain his wealth was precisely the way through which it became Yosef's. By investing his entire fortune in a single pearl, the gentile made the transfer of his wealth to Yosef as simple as could be.

This illustrates that God has infinite means through which to bring about a desired end. Those who see Shabbos obervance as a financial sacrifice would do well to bear this lesson in mind.

Ben Yehoyada writes that the סָבָא, *elder*, mentioned here [and in other Talmudic accounts] is Elijah the Prophet. Elijah was informing Yosef that the great reward he had received was for this specific act of purchasing the fish, rather than for the exceptional way in which he honored the Shabbos each week. The fish had been brought to the market late Friday afternoon. By the time Yosef had bought the fish, it was too late to begin cooking it. Yosef cut the fish open in order to preserve it for after Shabbos. He bought it out of concern that were he not to buy it, these fishermen might grow frustrated and no longer catch fish to sell to Jews for Shabbos. Thus, the great expense which Yosef undertook to buy this large fish was considered a 'loan' of sorts for the Shabbos, to ensure that it would be honored properly in the future. Thus did Elijah say, "To one who borrows for the Shabbos, the Shabbos pays back."

The Special Spice

هه The Talmud (*Shabbos* 119a) relates:

The Roman emperor asked R' Yehoshua ben Chananiah, "Why is it that your foods on the seventh day have such a wonderful aroma?" The sage replied: "It is because of a spice that we have — its name is Shabbos. Adding this spice is what causes the aroma."

"Give us some of it," demanded the emperor.

R' Yehoshua responded, "It is of benefit only to those who keep the Shabbos in accordance with all it laws. It will not help those who do not keep the Shabbos."

R' Yehoshua's words are to be taken literally: The spiritual aura of Shabbos manifests itself upon food that is cooked in honor of Shabbos. This manifestation is perceived tangibly, in the special aroma of Shabbos foods. The blessing that is readily discernible in the Shabbos food is an obvious illustration that this day is a gift to the Children of Israel and to no other nation. This is alluded to in the word תַּבְשִׁיל, *cooked dish*, whose letters can be rearranged to spell לִי שַׁבָּת, *Shabbos is mine (Ben Yehoyada)*.

To further amplify this point, R' Yosef Chaim of Baghdad[1] relates the following:

In the city of Baghdad, there lived a Jew who made known his intention to convert to Islam. According to government law, such a conversion was not recognized until the chief rabbi of the area met with the apostate and tried to convince him to remain a Jew. Should the rabbi fail in his attempt, the conversion would be declared valid by the government.

All arguments and persuasions that the rabbi could muster had no effect on the sinner. However, before their meeting had ended, a friend of the apostate appeared. Turning to the apostate, the friend said, "You and I both know how delectable the fragrant Shabbos food is to you. Remember, should you abandon the way of Torah, you will never again experience this pleasure, for it is a blessing that is conferred only upon food cooked in honor of the holy Shabbos."

These words had their desired effect and the man abandoned his plans.

---

1. Famed author of *Ben Ish Chai* and *Ben Yehoyada;* he was the leader of Sephardic Jewry in the early part of this century.

Pay Heed!

◄§ *Ben Yehoyada* sees significance in R' Yehoshua's description of this blessing as a תַּבְלִין, *spice*. He prefaces his explanation with the following anecdote:

A *tzaddik* decided to join his righteous peer for a Shabbos meal without invitation. As he was coming uninvited, the guest brought food along with him.[1] At the meal, the host was served a dish containing foods both from his own kitchen and that of his guest. The host exclaimed:

"The fragrance of your food is tenfold that of mine! Why?"

The guest replied: "My wife's lips are like roses, they drip with the fragrance of myrrh.[2] As my wife cooks, she expresses the feelings of her heart, that her actions are being done in honor of the holy Shabbos. This is the source of the fragrance of her food. Your food, however, is prepared by your servants, who cook without any thought at all."

The letters of the word תַּבְלִין, says *Ben Yehoyada*, form the words תְּנִי לֵב, *"Pay heed!"* — an exhortation to the women of the house to go about their Shabbos preparations mindful of the loftiness of their task.

Meat, Fish, and Wine

◄§ *Shulchan Aruch* (*Orach Chaim* 250:1) writes that one should prepare meat, wine, and delicacies in abundance for the first two Shabbos meals. *Mishnah Berurah* (242:2) adds that fish should be eaten at each of the three meals. Meat and wine are basic to Jewish festivity and celebration (*Pesachim* 109a), but what is the significance of fish?

The Chofetz Chaim (*Beur Halachah* 242:1, s.v. זכר למן), citing *Toras Chaim*, writes that the combination of meat, fish and wine is an allusion to the Day of Everlasting Shabbos (יוֹם שֶׁכֻּלּוֹ שַׁבָּת) of which the seventh day is a semblance (see p. 39). The *Midrash* relates that in Messianic times, God will host a feast for the righteous at which a giant fish known as the לִוְיָתָן, *Leviathan* (see *Bava Basra* 75a), and a giant animal referred to as the שׁוֹר הַבָּר, *Shor HaBor* (Wild Ox; see

---

1. Obviously, for the *tzaddik* to have carried his food the area must have been enclosed by an *eruv*.

2. Paraphrased from *Song of Songs* 5:13.

Psalms 50:11 with *Targum*), will be served. Also to be served at that meal is יֵין הַמְשׁוּמָר בַּעֲנָבָיו, *wine which has been preserved in its grapes* since the six days of Creation (*Berachos* 34b). The Shabbos meal is a semblance of that great feast of the future.

An additional reason for eating fish, writes *Ta'amei HaMinhagim*, is that the eyes of fish are always open, even when they sleep. In this, they are reminiscent of their Creator, Whose Providential eye is always open and observant. Since Shabbos is a testimony to God's existence and constant Providence, it is fitting to serve fish at the Shabbos meal.

Why does the meal customarily *begin* with fish? During the six days of Creation, the first living creatures to be created were fish (*Genesis* 1:21). Since the sanctity of Shabbos is the source from which not only blessing, but life itself flows,[1] we begin the Shabbos meal by partaking of the very first creature to have lived on this earth (*Ohr HaShabbos*).

A Tapestry of Sevens

◆§ In the world of Torah, the number seven denotes spiritual significance. This is even apparent in the number's mathematical properties. The following combination of properties is common only to the numbers one and seven: neither of these two numbers is the product of any two whole numbers other than itself and one; and neither is a prime factor of any other number between ten and one. Both one and seven represent the oneness of God and the spiritual essence with which He has infused creation (*The Wisdom in the Hebrew Alphabet*).

The unique spirituality of Shabbos is illustrated by the constant recurrence of the number seven in matters related to this lofty day. *Ba'al HaTurim* (*Exodus* 20:8) notes the following:

The opening verse of the *mitzvah* of Shabbos is the seventh in the Ten Commandments. The verse itself opens with the letter ז (which has a numerical value of seven): זָכוֹר אֶת יוֹם הַשַּׁבָּת לְקַדְּשׁוֹ.

The commandment lists seven for whom work is forbidden on the Shabbos: *You may do no work — you, your son and your daughter, your slave and your maidservant, your animal, and the stranger who is in your gates* (*ibid.* v. 10). Corresponding to this are the seven references to מְנוּחָה, *rest*, in the '*Atah Echad*' section of the Shabbos *Minchah*.

---

1. See comment from *Ohr HaChaim* on p. 51.

The *Vilna Gaon* observes that the מִסְפָּר קָטָן (digit sum) of the *gematria* of each item that is basic to the Shabbos table is seven:

גֵר (candle): נ = 50 ר = 200 50 + 200 = 250. 2 + 5 + 0 = 7

יַיִן (wine): י = 10 י = 10 ן = 50 10 + 10 + 50 = 70. 7 + 0 = 7

חַלָּה (challah): ח = 8 ל = 30 ה = 5 8 + 30 + 5 = 43. 4 + 3 = 7

דָּג (fish): ד = 4 ג = 3 4 + 3 = 7

בָּשָׂר (meat): ב = 2 שׂ = 300 ר = 200 2 + 300 + 200 = 502.
5 + 0 + 2 = 7

In Deed and Speech

◆§ The passage from *Isaiah* (58:13-14) cited earlier is the source for a number of other dicta pertaining to Shabbos. *Rambam* (*Hilchos Shabbos* 24:1) writes:

"There are practices which are forbidden on Shabbos although they are not even a semblance of a [forbidden] labor and will not lead to any labor. If so, why are they forbidden? Because it is written, *"If you restrain, because of the Shabbos, your feet, refrain from attending to your mundane needs on My holy day. . .and you honor it by not doing your own ways, from seeking your personal mundane needs or discussing the forbidden."*

From the above verse, the Sages derive:

[וְכִבַּדְתּוֹ] מֵעֲשׂוֹת דְּרָכֶיךָ, *[and you honor it] by not doing your own ways* — This teaches that even one's manner of walk should reflect the מְנוּחָה, *restful contentment*, of the Shabbos day. One should not run on Shabbos (except to perform a *mitzvah*), nor should one walk with unusually long strides. (See *Orach Chaim* 301.)

מִמְּצוֹא חֶפְצְךָ, *from seeking your mundane needs* — It is forbidden to plan matters of a mundane nature so that one will be able to do the necessary work once Shabbos has ended. For example, one cannot inspect his fields in order to ascertain what work will need to be done on Sunday. However, it is permitted to plan matters relevant to a *mitzvah*; for example, to make decisions regarding charity distributions that will take place after Shabbos, or to arrange a possible *shidduch*, marriage match. As the Sages put it: *"Your* needs are forbidden, but the needs of Heaven are permitted. (See *Orach Chaim* 306.)

וְדַבֵּר דָּבָר, *or discussing the forbidden* — It is forbidden to even mention on Shabbos one's intention of performing during the weekdays an act which is forbidden on Shabbos. (See *Orach Chaim* 307.)

What is the reward for adherence to all of the above? The prophet Isaiah continues (*Isaiah* 58:14):

Then you shall be granted pleasure with Hashem, for by making the Shabbos a day of delight, you will feel a sense of closeness to God, just as a son enjoys the company of his father (*Ibn Ezra*).

And I shall mount you astride the heights of the world, as you will be granted dominion over the Land of Israel which is described in Scripture as the earth's highest point (*Radak*).

And I shall provide you with the heritage of your father Jacob, which, in contrast to the blessings granted Abraham and Isaac, was without limitation or constraint of any sort (*Rashi*).

As God Rested

◆ While *Talmud Bavli* cites the above verse in *Isaiah* as the source for restricting one's speech on Shabbos, *Talmud Yerushalmi* (*Shabbos* 15:3) derives this from the Torah. We know that to effect Creation, God required no 'work,' in the common use of that term. Rather, He created the world through His utterances alone: *By the word of* HASHEM *the heaven was made, and by the breath of His mouth all their host* (*Psalms* 33:6). When the Torah states that *He abstained on the seventh day from all His work* (*Genesis* 2:2), the intent is that all such utterances ceased with the advent of Shabbos. Our observance of Shabbos as a day of restful contentment is meant to parallel that of God at the time of creation. It follows, then, that refraining from speaking of work is an integral aspect of proper Shabbos observance.[1]

In Accordance with His Deed

Whoever hallows the Shabbos as befits it, whoever protects the Shabbos properly from desecration, his reward is exceedingly great — in accordance with his deed (Sabbath Eve Zemiros).

---

1. The practice of engaging in forbidden discussions on Shabbos by prefacing one's remarks with the words *'nisht Shabbos g'ret'* ('not spoken on Shabbos') is, of course, contrary to *Halachah*.

◆§ The way in which people experience Shabbos can vary and the variance can be great indeed. *Whoever hallows the Shabbos as he befits it* refers to one who appreciates Shabbos for the spiritual paradise that it is. *Whoever protects the Shabbos from desecration* refers to those whose Shabbos observance is basically negative in nature, that is, they abstain from doing that which is forbidden but do not partake of the day's loftiness in a positive sense. Regarding each such Jew we can say, *"His reward is exceedingly great"* — but the reward will be *in accordance with his deed*, and will correspond exactly to the way in which this great *mitzvah* is performed (*Chofetz Chaim*).

This concept is actually alluded to in the Torah itself. With regard to the *mitzvah* of Shabbos, one verse states that for six days תַּעֲבֹד, *you shall work* (*Exodus* 20:9-10), while elsewhere (ibid. 35:2) the term תֵּעָשֶׂה מְלָאכָה, *work shall be done*, is used. Noting this discrepancy, *Mechilta* (ibid.) comments: "When the Jewish people fulfill the will of the Omnipresent, their work is done by others; however, when they do not fulfill His will, then their work is done by themselves." *Meshech Chochmah* (*Exodus* 31:16) adds that another discrepancy between these verses bears out *Mechilta's* point. The second verse says of Shabbos, יִהְיֶה לָכֶם קֹדֶשׁ, *it shall be hallowed unto you*. In the first verse, however, the word קֹדֶשׁ, *hallowed*, is not used. When a Jew fulfills the will of God in experiencing Shabbos in the desired manner, then he becomes suffused with the day's קְדוּשָׁה, *holiness*, thereby meriting that his work be done by others, so that he may further devote himself to lofty pursuits.

Entering the Day

Misplaced Haste

> *Seekers of HASHEM, seed of Abraham His beloved, who delay departing from the Shabbos and rush to enter. . .(Shabbos Eve Zemiros).*

◆§ The Chofetz Chaim commented: How unfortunate are those who delay in entering the Shabbos until the very last minute but hurry to depart from it as soon as they can! For the six days of work are rooted in the curse which God placed upon Adam after the latter partook of the Tree of Knowledge: *By the sweat of your brow shall you eat bread* (*Genesis* 3:19). Only the day of Shabbos was excluded from this curse, for *Elokim blessed the seventh day and hallowed it* (ibid. 2:3) — and Shabbos is the source of blessing for the entire week. Should we not be anxious to enter this wellspring of blessing and delay our departure from it?

Bride and Queen

[On Friday afternoon] R' Chanina would say: "Come, let us go to greet the Bride, the [Shabbos] Queen" (Bava Kamma 32a).

◆§ The Talmud teaches that as the Shabbos drew near, the Sages would don their finest clothing and make the same or similar pronouncement as that of R' Chanina above. A thousand years later, the Kabbalists of Safed embellished this Talmudic custom by actually walking out to the fields to 'welcome the Bride and Queen.' It was there, in Safed, that the קַבָּלַת שַׁבָּת, *welcoming the Shabbos*, service was first formulated, and from there it spread to the entire world.

Maharsha (*Chiddushei Agados*) explains the term כַּלָּה, *bride*, according to the *Midrash* (see p. 29) that the Jewish Nation is the בֶּן זוּג, *mate*, of the Shabbos. In this relationship, says *Maharsha*, Shabbos is the bride. Late Friday afternoon, when Shabbos begins, is comparable to the *chuppah* ceremony between groom and bride. Just as a groom steps forward to greet his bride as she walks toward the *chuppah* (canopy), so did the righteous of earlier generations go forth to welcome the Shabbos.

In the above Talmudic citation, R' Chanina refers to the Shabbos as both a כַּלָּה, *bride*, and a מַלְכְּתָא, *queen*. *Michtav Me'Eliyahu* relates these two terms to the dual aspects of the day: Shabbos is a queen in that it imbues those who keep it with its unique spiritual light. It is a bride in that it is enhanced by the aura of those who properly observe it (see p. 41).

Maharal explains these terms in a different light. A bride is distinct in her complete, deep-rooted attachment to her groom. A queen is distinct in her removal from and dominion over her subjects. The Shabbos is like a bride in that it is the means through which this mundane, corporeal world achieves an attachment with the spiritual world above. The day is also a queen with regard to the six days that precede it, for by way of its intrinsic holiness, the day of Shabbos is distinct and supreme.

A Proper Greeting

◆§ How does one properly ready himself to greet that which is both bride and queen? In *Mishnah Berurah* (250:3), the Chofetz Chaim writes: "The commentators state that on every *Erev Shabbos*, one should ponder thoughts of repentance and examine his deeds, for the Shabbos is called Bride and Queen, and [as Shabbos begins] it is as if one is going to greet royalty. It is improper to greet the Shabbos when clothed in rags of sin."

A Spirit of Brotherhood

◆§ *Yalkut Shimoni* relates that מִזְמוֹר שִׁיר לְיוֹם הַשַּׁבָּת, *A psalm, a song for the seventh day* (*Psalm* 92), was first recited by Adam. Adam ate from the Tree of Knowledge late Friday afternoon, the very day on which he had been created. As Shabbos arrived, death was decreed against Adam. However, the Shabbos came forward to serve as Adam's advocate. "Master of the universe," the Shabbos said, "during the six days of creation, no man was punished with death. Must such judgment begin today? Is this my sanctity? Is this my blessing?" God accepted the Shabbos' plea and Adam was spared.

Adam then began to sing, *"A psalm, a song for the seventh day. . ."* Said the Shabbos, "You are praising me? Let us both praise the Holy One; *it is good to praise Hashem. . ."* (ibid.).

From this *Midrash*, says R' Avraham Pam, we can derive that the sin of causing hurt or aggravation to one's fellow is especially grave if committed on Shabbos. Such behavior causes the Shabbos to come forth, as it were, and cry out, "Is this my sanctity? Is this my praise?"

When the Queen Reigns

◆§ A former maidservant in the house of R' Elimelech of Lizensk recalled, "During the week, angry words were often exchanged among the kitchen staff, as is apt to happen. But every Friday night, something strange would happen. We would embrace one another and say tearfullly, "Forgive me for whatever wrong I may have done during the week. *A gutten Shabbos*!"

In the house of a *tzaddik* such as R' Elimelech, the true spirit of Shabbos reigns. One can actually sense that this day is the goal of creation, a day that demands a standard of behavior that is above the norm. Where there exists a true spirit of Shabbos, there is no place for pettiness and strife (*Living Each Day*).

The Storm Before the Calm

◆§ Just as there is a *mitzvah* of *tosafos Shabbos*, that is, to add to Shabbos by ushering it in before sundown and concluding it after dark, so should one begin exercising extreme caution in his behavior toward others well before Shabbos has begun. *R' Pam* illustrates this point with an incident found in the Talmud (*Gittin* 62a): Two neighbors were incited by Satan every *Erev Shabbos* to quarrel with one another. Then the Tannaic sage R' Meir came to their neighborhood. He successfully restrained them from quarreling for three consecutive weeks and ultimately made peace between them. R' Meir listened as a frustrated Satan lamented over his having been evicted from a place where he had always found himself welcome.

It is not coincidental that Satan chose *Erev Shabbos* as the day for his weekly visits. The often frenzied activity prior to candle-lighting provides many opportunities for flare-ups and ill will. Furthermore, one might be deluded into believing that preparing for Shabbos is an excuse for saying or doing whatever one deems necessary for accomplishing his tasks.

It is for us to thwart Satan's designs and maintain our composure as we prepare for this lofty day.

Between Husband and Wife

◆§ The initial letters of בּוֹאוּ וְנֵצֵא לִקְרַאת שַׁבָּת מַלְכְּתָא, *Come, let us go to greet the Shabbos Queen*, form the word בְּשָׁלוֹם, *in peace*. To merit the spiritual blessings that descend with the arrival of Shabbos, peace and harmony must exist between man and his neighbor, and between husband and wife (*Ben Yehoyada*).

Mishnah Berurah (262:9) writes: "*Zohar* and the Kabbalists caution exceedingly against any sort of strife, God forbid, on Shabbos — especially between husband and wife."

Candle-Lighting

◆§ The Sages ordained that Shabbos be ushered in with the lighting of candles by the woman of the house. Inherent in this *mitzvah* are both *kavod* (honor of) and *oneg* (delight to) *Shabbos* (see pp. 57-59). The Talmud (*Shabbos* 25a) states that candle-lighting also enhances *shalom bayis*, household harmony, for a properly lit home provides a tranquil atmosphere. It is perhaps in keeping with this spirit of peace that is so crucial to the Shabbos that (as stated in *Tikkunei Zohar*) the husband customarily prepares the candles for his wife.[1]

The *Midrash* (*Yalkut Shimoni, Beha'alosecha* 8) states that in the merit of candle-lighting, the Jewish People will bask in the Divine light at the time of the Redemption. The Talmud (*Shabbos* 23b) teaches that through fulfillment of this *mitzvah*, one can merit sons who will grow to become Torah scholars. As it is written, *for a mitzvah is a candle and Torah is light* (*Proverbs* 6:23); through the *mitzvah* of the Shabbos candles, the light of Torah will be manifest in one's children (*Rashi, Shabbos* 23b).

Mishnah Berurah (263:2) writes, "It is fitting for a woman to pray after lighting the Shabbos candles. The blessing [which she should seek] is that the Holy One grant her sons who will shine with [the light of] Torah."

Zohar (I, 48b) states: "A woman needs to be glad of heart when she kindles the Shabbos lights, for it is a great honor and a great source of merit for her to have holy sons who will shine with Torah and fear of Heaven, and who will increase peace in the world. She will also cause her husband's days and years to be lengthened. Therefore, she must be meticulous in [performing] this *mitzvah*."

Kitzur Shulchan Aruch (75:2) writes that it is proper for a woman to give *tzedakah* before lighting the candles.

Blessing of the Children

◆§ *Sforno* (*Genesis* 32:1) comments that the Torah makes mention of Laban's blessing to his daughters to teach that the blessing of a father to his children — whoever the father might be — is given with all his soul and is therefore particularly effective. The flow of sanctity and Divine beneficence which comes with the beginning of Shabbos makes that time particularly auspicious for such blessings.

---

1. The *Mishnah* (*Shabbos* 2:6) stresses the need for a woman to be meticulous in *mitzvos* of נִדָּה, חַלָּה וְהַדְלָקַת הַנֵּר, *family purity, challah, and kindling the Shabbos light[s]*. It would seem that the text should have read, נִדָּה, חַלָּה, וְנֵר, *family purity, challah, and Shabbos light[s]*. R' Akiva Eiger sees the *Mishnah's* wording as indicating that the woman's *mitzvah* is to *kindle* the Shabbos lights, while her husband should prepare them.

It is customary to bless one's children, young and old, either in the synagogue after the *Ma'ariv* service or upon returning home. The standard text of this blessing incorporates the verses of *Bircas Kohanim*, the Priestly Blessing, as found in *Numbers* (6:24-26). These verses are preceded, for a boy, by the words יְשִׂמְךָ אֱלֹקִים כְּאֶפְרַיִם וְכִמְנַשֶּׁה, *May God make you like Ephraim and Menashe* (*Genesis* 48:20); and for a girl by the words יְשִׂמֵךְ אֱלֹקִים כְּשָׂרָה רִבְקָה רָחֵל וְלֵאָה, *May God make you like Sarah, Rebecca, Rachel, and Leah*. Each parent may add his own blessings as he sees fit (*Beis Yaakov*). The blessing should be conferred with both hands resting upon the child's head to signify that the blessing is conveyed with complete generosity of spirit.

Besamim Rosh comments: "The principle is that one bless his children that he merit to raise them to Torah, marriage and good deeds; that they be truly God fearing with no ulterior motives but with complete sincerity; that they live long lives dedicated to the service of God and to His Torah in utter truth; that they have children and grandchildren who will engage sincerely in Torah and the commandments; and that they merit both tables [i.e., spiritual and material wealth] according to God's abundant compassion and loving-kindness without limit."

Shalom Aleichem

◄§ The *Shalom Aleichem* song, sung upon returning home from the synagogue on Shabbos eve, is based on the following Talmudic passage:

"Two ministering angels — one good and one evil — escort a person home from the synagogue on the eve of Shabbos. If a Jew arrives home and finds a burning lamp, a set table, and a made bed, the good angel says, 'May it be God's will that it also be so next Shabbos.' The evil angel is compelled to answer, 'Amen.' But if not — then the evil angel says, 'May it be God's will that it also be so next Shabbos.' The good angel is compelled to answer, 'Amen'" (*Shabbos* 119b).

The song consists of four stanzas. In the first we speak of מַלְאֲכֵי הַשָּׁרֵת, *ministering angels*. However, the next three stanzas speak of מַלְאֲכֵי הַשָּׁלוֹם, *angels of peace*. In the first stanza, we greet the entire heavenly host which stands in the service of God. In the next three stanzas, we address those angels who accompany us home on Shabbos eve (*R' Isaac of Komarna*).

The third stanza begins: בָּרְכוּנִי לְשָׁלוֹם, *Bless me for peace*. Of course, the source of man's blessing is in his actions, not in the good will of angels; to the contrary, angels for good or evil are created according to man's deeds. Moreover, it is forbidden to pray to angels (*Yerushalmi* 93:1). The request here must be understood in the context of the Talmudic passage cited above. It is an expression of hope that the angels who have accompanied us home will be pleased with our Shabbos preparations, so that they will extend the blessing that it be equally so the following week.

The last stanza begins: צֵאתְכֶם לְשָׁלוֹם, *May your departure be to peace [O angels of peace]*. It seems difficult to understand why we are bidding farewell to the angels when they have just arrived.

Machatzis HaShekel explains that we are expressing a hope that whenever the angels choose to leave they should leave in peace, without accusation for any shortcomings they may have found in us.

K'lil Tiferes writes that a Jew is forever escorted by angels who are created through the *mitzvos* that he performs. However, the additional soul with which each Jew is endowed on Shabbos requires that the angels who accompany him on this day be of a higher order. Therefore, in the first stanza of the song, we welcome the angels that have come to escort us on Shabbos, while in the final stanza, we take leave of those angels who have been with us throughout the week.

An Accomplished Woman

> R' Yitzchak ben Nechemiah said: Just as God gave the Torah to Israel by means of the twenty-two letters [of the Aleph-Beis], so does He praise righteous women by means of the twenty-two letters (*Yalkut Mishlei* ch. 31).

◆§ *Aishes Chayil*, 'An Accomplished Woman,' which is customarily sung prior to the Shabbos Eve *Kiddush*, consists of the final twenty-two verses of *Proverbs*. The verses' initial letters are the twenty-two letters of the *Aleph-Beis* in consecutive order. The commentators agree that the chapter is allegorical. It is variously interpreted as a reference to the *Shechinah*, Shabbos, the Torah, wisdom and the soul.

Shulchan HaTahor writes that one whose deeds and thoughts during the past week have been directed toward the service of God will experience an aura of holiness as he sings the praises of the *Shechinah* with this song on Friday night.

In its simple meaning, *Aishes Chayil* clearly describes the virtues of the accomplished woman who is the mainstay of her home. The fact that the Jewish woman was chosen as the vehicle for describing the lofty spiritual concepts listed above is in itself a profound tribute to her.

Midrash Tanchuma (*Genesis* ch. 23) interprets *Aishes Chayil* as Abraham's eulogy of Sarah, while *Midrash Mishlei* interprets the respective verses as references to righteous heroines of Jewish history.

A Shabbos Choice in the Warsaw Ghetto

◦§ In the Warsaw Ghetto, food rations for the entire week were distributed on Monday. The Nazis' inhuman plan was simple: Give the Jews all their food for the week at one time. Starving and suffering, many of them would find themselves unable to divide their minuscule allotments into seven portions. The food would be gone before the week's end, leaving them nothing for Shabbos. The holy day would be spent in hunger at best, in death through starvation at worst.

In one particular home, a sick child turned to his mother and said, "Mama, you made such a wonderful *kugel* last Shabbos! Could you please make one again for this coming Shabbos? Please, Mama!"

The child did not know that the main ingredient of the *kugel* had been the little pieces from his mother's own weekday rations that she had set aside in honor of the Seventh Day. Could she make the sacrifice again? How could she not, when her efforts would bring such joy to her little boy as well as to the Shabbos Queen?

This time, she added potato peelings to her crumbs. The peelings were ground into a flour, which was liberally seasoned with spices for flavoring. The mixture was ready to be popped into the oven, when a thought entered the woman's mind.

She had a few drops of oil saved in a jar. Those few drops would drastically improve the quality and taste of her dish. How delighted her sick little boy would be! It would bring nourishment to his shriveled body and delight to his pure little heart.

But how could she? She had been saving those few drops for fuel for the Shabbos candles. She knew that the *Halachah* placed the lighting of Shabbos candles ahead of delicacies in honor of Shabbos. She knew also that the moments after candle-lighting were most opportune for a mother to pray on behalf of her children. What better way to help her child than by praying for him as she kindled the Shabbos *lecht?*

But her motherly instinct would not permit her to place the *kugel* in the oven without that special ingredient. Her quandary continued — until she had an idea.

The oil was added to the mixture. Friday before sundown, the mother stood before her candles — wicks without oil. She said, "Master of the universe, please accept these candles without light. In Your infinite mercy, illuminate them with your Heavenly radiance. Forgive me for having stolen the oil from the wicks in order to light the joy of Shabbos in the hearts of my starving children. If I have sinned and You cannot accept this prayer, I beg of You, O Compassionate One, listen to the Shabbos songs of the children that will resound in my poor dwelling when I bring this *kugel* to the table."

That night, the children ate their *kugel*, which tasted of Paradise. They burst into song, "We will sing the song of Shabbos." The Shabbos Queen responded in kind, "Let us sing a song to the Jewish mother" (*R' Moshe Prager*).

Kiddush

◆§ It is from the verse זָכוֹר אֶת יוֹם הַשַּׁבָּת לְקַדְּשׁוֹ, *Remember the Shabbos day to sanctify it (Exodus* 20:8), that we derive the requirement to sanctify the Shabbos through a verbal proclamation as the day arrives (*Sifra, Bechukosai* 1). This proclamation is known as *Kiddush,* Sanctification. Also derived from here is that the day should be sanctified verbally at its conclusion through the recital of *Havdalah,* Separation. Most commentators agree that the Scriptural mandate to proclaim the sanctity of Shabbos is fulfilled by reciting the relevant passages of *Shemoneh Esrei.* The further command to recite *Kiddush* again over a cup of wine, the beverage which gladdens the heart, is rabbinic in origin (see *Magen Avraham* to *Orach Chaim* 271:2).

The *Kiddush* of Shabbos morning was introduced by the Sages and as such, is inferior to the Shabbos Eve *Kiddush* whose origin is in the Torah. The morning *Kiddush* is euphemistically called קִידוּשָׁא רַבָּא, the 'Great' *Kiddush*, in the same sense that a sightless person is referred to in the Talmud as a סַגִּי נְהוֹר, *much vision* or *light.*

In explaining the significance of *Kiddush, Sefer HaChinuch* (§31) writes:

"Among the roots of this *mitzvah* is that we should become awakened through its performance to remember the greatness of this day and to set firmly in our hearts the concept of creation, *For in six days HASHEM created heaven and earth. . .* (*Exodus* 31:17). It is thus that we are obligated to perform this act with wine, for it is natural for one to become aroused through wine as it satisfies and gladdens — and as I have already said,[1] in accordance with one's actions and awakening [regarding a given matter] is he influenced toward that matter forever."

The Shabbos Prayers

A Trilogy of Sabbaths

⋅§ Whereas there is a uniform *Shemoneh Esrei* text for the *Shacharis*, *Minchah*, and *Ma'ariv* prayers of *Yom Tov*, such is not the case with Shabbos. On Shabbos, each *Shemoneh Esrei* has its own fourth blessing, the one which speaks of the Shabbos day. *Tur* (*Orach Chaim* 292) explains that each of the Shabbos prayers corresponds to a different aspect of Shabbos:

Ma'ariv

אַתָּה קִדַּשְׁתָּ אֶת יוֹם הַשְּׁבִיעִי לִשְׁמֶךְ תַּכְלִית מַעֲשֵׂה שָׁמַיִם וָאָרֶץ . . .
You sanctified the seventh day for Your Name's sake, the conclusion of the creation of heaven and earth. . .

⋅§ This prayer attests to the basic concept of Shabbos, a testimony to God's creation of the universe in six days, and His having abstained from creation on the seventh.

Shacharis

יִשְׂמַח מֹשֶׁה בְּמַתְּנַת חֶלְקוֹ כִּי עֶבֶד נֶאֱמָן קָרָאתָ לּוֹ . . . וּשְׁנֵי לוּחוֹת אֲבָנִים הוֹרִיד בְּיָדוֹ וְכָתוּב בָּהֶם שְׁמִירַת שַׁבָּת.
Moses rejoiced in the gift of his portion: that You called him a

---

1. *Mitzvah* 16.

faithful servant. . .He brought down two stone tablets in his hands, on which is inscribed the observance of the Shabbos.

ↇ The profound relationship between Shabbos and Torah, says *Tur*, is evident in that the Torah was given on Shabbos (*Shabbos* 86b).[1] Because the Torah was presented in the early morning hours (*Exodus* 19:16), mention of this is made in the Shabbos morning prayers.

Minchah

אַתָּה אֶחָד וְשִׁמְךָ אֶחָד וּמִי כְּעַמְּךָ יִשְׂרָאֵל גּוֹי אֶחָד בָּאָרֶץ.
You are One and Your Name is One; and who is like Your people Israel, one nation on earth.

ↇ This verse is a clear reference to *Zechariah* 14:9 which states that at the time of the Final Redemption, all the world will recognize the Oneness of God. According to *Kabbalah*, the Shabbos *Minchah* alludes to the יוֹם שֶׁכֻּלוֹ שַׁבָּת, *Day of Everlasting Shabbos,* of Messianic times.

Shabbos and the Festivals

ↇ In *Parashas Emor* (*Leviticus* ch.23), the chapter of the festivals is preceded by the mention of Shabbos. *Rashi* writes that this is to teach that whoever observes the Festivals is considered as if he has observed the Shabbos and whoever desecrates the Festivals is considered as if he has desecrated the Shabbos. R' Gedalyah Schorr (in *Ohr Gedalyahu*) writes that Shabbos encompasses within it the three festivals of Pesach, Shavuos and Succos and that each of these Festivals is associated with a different stage of the Shabbos.

Pesach symbolizes the swiftness with which a Jew can be transformed spiritually. From the forty-ninth level of impurity, the Children of Israel rose to the level of prophets at the Splitting of the Sea. (Alluding to the incredible swiftness of this transformation was the requirement that the Pesach offering be eaten in haste [*Exodus* 12:11].)

Every week as Shabbos begins, a Jew undergoes a similar transformation. As the sun sets late Friday afternoon, a Jew crosses the threshold from the world of the mundane and enters a world that

---

1. Further illustrative of this relationship is the teaching that one who keeps Shabbos is considered as if he has kept the entire Torah (*Talmud Yerushalmi, Nedarim* ch.3).

is spiritual. In discussing this, *Ohr Gedalyahu* cites the *Midrash* (*Shir HaShirim Rabbah* 4:17) which likens the Jewish people to a rooster that rolls in the dust and then cleans itself with a single flap of its wings. Similarly, each week a Jew shakes himself free of the world around him and rises to a level that grants him entrance into the world of Shabbos. This ability to attach oneself to the sanctity of Shabbos was granted our people at the time of the Exodus when the nation went from servitude to the status of the Chosen People.[1]

Shavuos is the Festival of the giving of the Torah, and, as mentioned above, the *Shacharis* service of Shabbos refers to that event, which occurred on Shabbos. *Pirkei D'R'Eliezer* writes that each Shabbos, Moses returns to the Jewish People the two crowns that were presented them at the giving of the Torah and which were forfeited due to the Sin of the Golden Calf. Thus, every Shabbos is a *matan* [giving of] *Torah* of sorts, a time that is most opportune for renewing one's dedication to Torah study. Moreover, just as Shavuos is preceded by the purifying days of *Sefirah*, when a Jew cleanses himself spiritually in preparation for receiving the Torah, so should a Jew strive during the night of Shabbos to ready himself for the added sanctity that descends on the morning of Shabbos and is manifest even more as the day progresses.

Succos, more than the other two Festivals, is related to the Final Redemption. *Radak* (*Zechariah* 14:16) writes that the cataclysmic battles of Gog and Magog that will precede the Redemption will occur at the time of Succos (which is why the *Haftarah* of the first day of Succos speaks of those battles). *Rashi* writes that those nations which will survive the battles of Gog and Magog will join Israel each year in celebrating the Succos festival.

Additionally, the Talmud (*Avodah Zarah* 3a) states that at the time of the Redemption, the *mitzvah* of *succah* will be used to prove that the gentile nations have no affinity for God's commandments and deserve no reward.

As mentioned above, the *Minchah* service of Shabbos alludes to the future Redemption. The *Shalosh Seudos* meal which follows is a time when God is most disposed toward His people and it is most opportune for beseeching Him to hasten the Final Redemption.

Ohr Gedalyahu concludes: "Thus, Shabbos encompasses within it these three aspects of *kedushah*, sanctity. We find that the word הַיּוֹם, *today*, is written three times regarding Shabbos (*Exodus* 16:25).

---

1. See p. 31.

Therefore, our Sages ordained that we eat three meals on the Shabbos (*Shabbos* 119b), for the day is actually three days in one and each day requires a meal for itself."

Moses' Joy

יִשְׂמַח מֹשֶׁה בְּמַתְּנַת חֶלְקוֹ.

Moses rejoiced in the gift of his portion (Shacharis Shemoneh Esrei).

✦ As cited above, *Pirkei D'R'Eliezer* writes that on each Shabbos, Moses returns to the Jewish People the two spiritual crowns that were presented by God at the time the Torah was given but which were subsequently forfeited after the Sin of the Golden Calf. Now, when one gives a gift, he is hopeful that the recipient will make good use of it; otherwise, the giver has no pleasure from his generosity. Each Shabbos, we pray that we will be worthy of utilizing the day of Shabbos properly, so that Moses will truly rejoice in his gift to us (*Siach Sarfei Kodesh*).

Faithful Servant

✦ The *Midrash* relates Moses' joy to the Shabbos itself. As a young man growing up in the palace of Pharaoh, Moses beheld the hard labor of his brethren. His heart was deeply pained and he pondered how to ease their plight. He approached the Egyptian king and said, "Your slaves are overworked and will soon collapse under the strain of their labor. It is in *your* interest to grant them one day off each week, so that their strength will be renewed and they will better serve you." Pharaoh accepted this argument and assigned Moses to select one day of the week as the Jews' day of rest. Moses chose the seventh day. When, years later, God commanded the nation regarding Shabbos, Moses realized that he had anticipated this command years before, and his heart became filled with joy. Therefore, we say: "Moses rejoiced in the gift of *his* portion."[1]

Lest anyone think that Moses' achievement might have led him to claim Divine powers, ח"ו, we continue: כִּי עֶבֶד נֶאֱמָן קָרָאתָ לּוֹ, *that You*

---

1. *Tur* (§292) cites an explanation of Moses' joy in relation to Shabbos based on the Talmudic passage (*Beitzah* 16a) where God told Moses, "I have a precious gift in my treasure house; its name is Shabbos and I desire to bestow it upon them [the Jews]. Go inform them of this." Upon hearing this, Moses rejoiced. (See p. 29.)

called him a faithful servant. This is a reference to *Numbers* 12:7, where Moses is described as a faithful servant. *Yalkut Shimoni* there offers a parable: A wealthy man purchased some fields and conferred their produce upon a third party. The purchaser's friends warned him, "If you allow that fellow full possession of the field's produce, he will in time claim that the field is his own." The man replied, "I trust this person completely; he will never claim such a thing."

Similarly, God associated Moses' name with the Torah itself, as it is written, *Remember the Torah of My servant Moses (Malachi* 3:22). Because Moses was so faithful a servant, God was willing to confer upon him the highest of accolades (*The World of Prayer*).

Shabbos and Torah

'You Are My Witnesses'

As mentioned above, the *Shacharis Shemoneh Esrei* of Shabbos alludes to the relationship between Shabbos and Torah.

Tanna D'Vei Eliyahu (ch.1, cited in *Tur* §290) relates: "The Torah came before the Holy One and said: 'When Israel will enter its Land, this one will run to his vineyard, that one will run to his field — and what will be with me?!' The Holy One replied: 'I have a mate with which I shall pair you. Its name is Shabbos. On this day, they [the Jewish People] will be free from work and will enter their houses of study and toil in Torah.'"

The above *Midrash* refers to Shabbos as the בֶּן זוּג, *mate*, of the Torah. Another *Midrash* (see p. 29) refers to the Jewish People as the בֶּן זוּג of the Shabbos. Thus, Shabbos, Torah and the Jewish People are firmly intertwined.

Parashas Vayakhel (*Exodus* 35) tells of Moses assembling the Congregation of Israel to relate God's command regarding the construction of the *Mishkan* (Tabernacle). By Divine Command, Moses prefaced these instructions with yet another exhortation to keep the Shabbos. *Midrash Tanchuma* there relates: The masters of *Aggadah* said: "From the beginning of the Torah until its end, there is no section that opens with [the term] קְהִלָּה, *assemblage,* save for this one. And why? Because the Holy One told Moses,

'Descend [from the Heavens] and make for me huge assemblages on Shabbos, so that all succeeding generations will learn to assemble on every Shabbos and enter the houses of study to teach Torah to the masses.' "

Tanchuma states further: Said the Holy One to Israel: "If you will assemble on every Shabbos to study Torah and the works of the prophets, I will consider it as if you have made Me King in My world, as the prophet said, *'You are My witnesses, vows* Hashem' *(Isaiah* 43:10) — You bear witness for Me that I am God in this world."

Beis Yoser (Tur §290) writes that the above *Midrash* is the source for the practice "wherever Jews are found, to gather in houses of prayer and study after the Shabbos morning meal, in order to study Scripture and to expound upon the teachings of *Aggadah*." *Bach* (ibid.) adduces from the language of *Tur* that the prime focus should be the study of *Halachah* — particularly the laws of Shabbos. *Bach* adds that the lecturer should also draw close the hearts of his listeners with Aggadic teachings that will inspire them to repentance and awe of Heaven, and will restrain them from sin.

Potent Study

ᴥᴥ§ *Ben Ish Chai* states: "The Kabbalists have stated that that which is accomplished through the study of Torah on Shabbos is one thousandfold that of Torah study on a weekday."

Sefer Kedushas HaShabbos[1] cites an early commentator who writes: "The day of Shabbos is most appropriate for the study of Torah, for the additional soul with which each person is endowed on Shabbos is an aid to all those who seek to know Torah."

One Friday night, after propounding a Torah insight, the *Chazon Ish* remarked, "Only on Shabbos, when endowed with a *neshamah yeseirah* (additional soul), can one fully appreciate this *chiddush*."

---

1. By Rabbi D. Sputz.

Favor of Favors

'And Who Is Like Your People. . .'

אַתָּה אֶחָד וְשִׁמְךָ אֶחָד וּמִי כְּעַמְּךָ יִשְׂרָאֵל גּוֹי אֶחָד בָּאָרֶץ.

You are One and Your Name is One; and who is like Your people Israel, one nation on earth (Minchah Shemoneh Esrei).

◄§ *Tosafos* (*Chagigah* 3b) comments that these words of the *Minchah* service allude to the following *Midrash*: "Three bear witness to one another: Israel, Shabbos, and the Holy One. Israel and the Holy One bear witness that Shabbos is a day of restful contentment; Israel and Shabbos bear witness that God is One; and the Holy One and Shabbos bear witness that Israel is singular among the nations."

Prior to the Torah reading of the Shabbos *Minchah* service, the congregation recites a verse (*Psalms* 69:14) which speaks of prayer being offered at an עֵת רָצוֹן, *opportune time*. The significance of this is reflected in the words of *Zohar*: "On the day of Shabbos, when the time for the *Minchah* prayer arrives, a favor of favors is to be found, and the Ancient Holiest of all reveals His will. . ." As mentioned above, the spiritual attachment which Israel attains with God on Shabbos reaches its zenith as the day nears its end. It is the time of *yichud*, unity, as it were, between God and His Chosen People (*Nesivos Shalom*), a time when He ushers His beloved nation into His inner sanctum (*Toras Avos*). It is therefore a most opportune time for prayer and a most fitting moment to make mention of the profound relationship between God, Israel, and the day of Shabbos.

Shalosh Seudos

R' Yose said: "May my portion be among those who eat three meals on the Shabbos" (Shabbos 118b).

Whoever observes the three meals [of Shabbos] will be spared from three tribulations: the birthpangs of the Messianic era, the judgment of Gehinnom, and the War of Gog and Magog (Shabbos 118a).

◄§ Those who observe the three meals have brought delight to the Shabbos in the desired manner. In this merit, they will be spared the sufferings that will precede the Day of Everlasting Shabbos, of which Shabbos is a semblance (*Maharsha* ibid.).

The Third Meal is universally referred to as *Shalosh Seudos*, literally *Three Meals*. *Divrei Emes* explains that the first two Shabbos meals are eaten at normal mealtimes. Thus it is not obvious that the food at those meals is being consumed in honor of Shabbos. But the Third Meal is held at a time of day when many people are not at all hungry; in fact, they would probably not be eating at all were it not a *mitzvah* to do so. Thus, their eating of this meal lends significance to the previous two as well, as it demonstrates that they partake of the Sabbath meals not because the food tempts them, but because God commanded that they eat. Therefore, this third meal is known as *Shalosh Seudos*.

Taking Leave

◄§ As we have seen, the late afternoon of Shabbos is known in Kabbalistic literature as רַעֲוָא דְרַעֲוִין, the *[time of]* favor of favors, i.e., a time when God is most favorably disposed toward Israel, thus making it most opportune for arousing the Heavenly Attribute of Mercy toward our people.

Chiddushei HaRim explains *Shalosh Seudos* as an expression of קָשָׁה עָלַי פְּרֵידַתְכֶם, *your leave-taking is hard for me*, for the Shabbos and one's additional soul is about to take leave. As we take part in *Shalosh Seudos*, we are demonstrating how very precious each moment of Shabbos is, how we savor it, and how we hope that our experiencing of the current Shabbos will infuse us with added sanctity for the week ahead.

It is customary, especially among *Chassidim* whose literature contains much regarding *Shalosh Seudos*, to spend the meal in the company of many others and to enhance it with abundant *zemiros* and words of Torah.

A Time to Beseech

◄§ *Toras Avos* explains the significance of *Shalosh Seudos*, and its accompanying heartfelt *zemiros*, with a parable:

A king had a son who desired to ask much of his father but feared rejection. One day, the king's beloved confidant visited the palace. The son hosted a number of festive meals for his father's friend and became very close to him. When it came time for the confidant to go on his way, the son approached him privately and asked that he speak to the king for him.

"Why have you waited until now to ask this of me?" the confidant demanded.

The son replied, "I felt it improper to mar your visit by unburdening myself to you. However, now that you are about to leave, I must ask you to speak on my behalf."

Shabbos is the King's beloved, the most coveted of days. Throughout Shabbos we rejoice, putting aside our worries as we honor and give delight to the day. However, at the time of *Shalosh Seudos*, when the day is soon to depart, we seize the moment and plead for the sake of our nation.

Melaveh Malkah

Escorting the Queen

One should always arrange his table on Motza'ei Shabbos [i.e., after the conclusion of Shabbos], even though he desires to eat only a small amount, in order to honor [the Shabbos] when it leaves. Warm drink on Motza'ei Shabbos is curative, warm bread on Motza'ei Shabbos is curative (Shabbos 119b).

⋙ A visiting monarch is ushered in and escorted out. The Shabbos Queen is escorted out with the meal known as *Melaveh Malkah,* literally, Escorting the Queen.

Chapter 300 of both *Tur* and *Shulchan Aruch* (*Orach Chaim*) reads: "A person should always prepare his table on *Motza'ei Shabbos* in order to escort the Shabbos, even if all he needs to eat is a *k'zayis*." That this law is accorded a chapter of its own underscores the importance of the *Melaveh Malkah* meal (*Chozeh of Lublin*).[1]

---

1. The *Chozeh* made the same observation regarding the importance of honoring *Rosh Chodesh* with a proper meal (see *Orach Chaim* 419).

Nourishment for the Future

◄§ The early commentators have taught that there is a limb in the human anatomy called *naskoy*[1] which remains intact in the grave — even after the rest of the body has decomposed — until the Resurrection of the Dead in the future. It is around this limb that each body will recompose and come back to life. This limb derives nourishment from nothing but the *Melaveh Malkah* meal (based on *Mishnah Berurah* 300:1).

Meal of King David

◄§ *Melaveh Malkah* is described as the meal of King David. This description has its roots in the events surrounding David's death, as recorded in the Talmud (*Shabbos* 30a). It was revealed to King David that he would die on Shabbos — but not which Shabbos. Therefore, whenever he survived a Shabbos, it was cause for rejoicing, for himself and the entire Jewish Nation. In commemoration, we celebrate the evening with סְעוּדָתָא דְּדָוִד מַלְכָּא מְשִׁיחָא, *the Meal of David, the Anointed King*.

It may be, too, that because David was the נְעִים זְמִירוֹת יִשְׂרָאֵל, *Sweet Singer of Israel*, his meal is celebrated with abundant *zemiros* (*Ziv HaShabbos*).

Elijah the Prophet

◄§ A central place in the *Melaveh Malkah zemiros* is held for the prophet Elijah. *Tur* (*Orach Chaim* 295) writes:

"It is customary to mention Elijah the Prophet [on *Motza'ei Shabbos*]. *Ba'al Halttur* explains that this is because Elijah is destined to herald the Redemption. The Talmud (*Eruvin* 43b) states: 'Israel is assured that Elijah will appear neither on an *Erev Shabbos* nor on an *Erev Yom Tov*.'[2] Therefore, once Shabbos has

---

1. Also known as *luz* (see *Mateh Moshe* §513).

2. This is because people would naturally drop whatever they were doing and go out to greet Elijah, leaving the preparations for Shabbos and *Yom Tov* unfinished (*Rashi*, ibid.). Elijah cannot appear on Shabbos because, as the Talmud there states, the laws of *techum Shabbos* (which limit the distance one may travel on Shabbos) make this impossible.

passed and it is now possible that he will appear, we pray that he come."[1]

Maharil (quoting *Rosh*) cites a *Tosefta* that Elijah enters the Garden of Eden every *Motza'ei Shabbos* and records the praises of Shabbos observers.

Stories of Self-Sacrifice

Ariel

◄§ For many generations, there lived a family in the city of Hebron by the surname אֲרִיאֵל, *Ariel*. The word אֲרִיאֵל is a contraction of אֲרִי אֵל, *lion of God*. It is told that the family got its name from the following story:

A few hundred years ago, a family ancestor was designated by his community to undertake a mission of mercy on behalf of the community poor. The man, who was revered for both his piety and scholarship,[2] was to travel to a wealthy Jewish community in a distant land and hopefully inspire them to come to the aid of their impoverished brethren.

As the path of his journey would take him through a wilderness which was fraught with danger, the man joined a caravan of gentile travelers who were heading toward the same destination. Before the caravan departed, the man told the caravan leader that as a Jew, he could not travel on Shabbos. He requested that the caravan members respect his requirement to refrain from travel on that day, and he offered a generous sum of money to make up for any possible loss or discomfort that the travelers might suffer because of this. The leader happily accepted the money and promised to honor the Jew's request.

When Friday afternoon arrived, the Jew reminded the leader of

---

1. In a succeeding chapter (299), *Tur* cites a custom to recite on *Motza'ei Shabbos* all Scriptural verses in which Elijah is mentioned. *Tur* continues, "They say that it is good [i.e., auspicious] for [preventing] forgetfulness and for insuring success in one's endeavors in the forthcoming week."

2. Some say that this man was R' Shimon ibn Lavi, who composed the famous *Bar Yochai* song. The Hebrew word לָבִיא, *lavi*, means *awesome lion*.

their discussion. The man responded with sardonic laughter, saying that he had no intention of delaying an entire caravan because of the whims of a single individual, let alone a Jew.

The Jew was in a quandary. The caravan was then in the wilderness, the only signs of life being those of beasts of prey. To remain would be to place his life in obvious danger. To leave would be to desecrate Shabbos, though through no fault of his own.

He was left with no choice, for while he mulled over his predicament, the caravan continued on without him. He was all alone.

As Shabbos approached, the man spread out a sheet on the ground, set up two candlesticks and lit two candles. He prayed the Shabbos Eve prayers, recited *Kiddush*, and proceeded with a very simple Shabbos meal. He began to sing *zemiros*, oblivious to the dangers all around him. Suddenly, the man heard an unmistakable roar. He looked up and found himself face to face with a lion. However, the lion made no attempt to attack. Rather, it placed itself alongside the man and settled down as would any domestic pet. With the candles still lit, the man continued with his Shabbos meal as his newfound friend looked on. At the conclusion of his meal, the man settled down to sleep, as the lion remained near him keeping watch. When he awoke the next morning, the lion was gone, but it reappeared again as the man began his daytime meal. The lion remained lying at the man's side until the stars appeared and Shabbos drew to a close.

At that point, the lion stood up, walked in front of the man and crouched before him as would a camel waiting for its master to mount. As soon as the man had settled himself on the lion, it took off — along the exact path that the man's journey was to take him! By morning, the lion had overtaken the caravan that had left the man stranded. Pulling up alongside the caravan leader, the lion crouched again to discharge its passenger. It then turned around and disappeared into the wilderness whence it had come, as the travelers looked on in awe and disbelief.

The gentiles fell to their knees in front of the Jew begging forgiveness for having forsaken him. From that moment on, he was treated as a king, until arriving safely at his destination.

The Test

❧ When vacationing at a resort, Rabbi Dr. Marcus Lehman met an aged Jew from the Netherlands who related the following:

The man had owned a highly successful carpet business in the Hague. Among his steady customers was the land's royal family.

One Shabbos Eve, the man and his family were singing *zemiros* as they sat around the Shabbos table, when there was a knock on the door. A messenger of Crown Prince Hendrick had come to request that a shipment of expensive carpets be sent to the royal palace at once. The Jew replied that he did not conduct business on Shabbos. The messenger responded that the carpets were needed for a party that the prince was throwing that very night. The Jew responded that, while he well understood the urgency of the matter, his religious beliefs made it impossible for him to honor the prince's request.

The messenger returned twice more that night. The last time, he came with a written request penned by the prince himself. The request ended with a threat that the Jew would suffer severely were he to ignore the order. Again, the Jew apologized, but stood firm. He knew that current law would not permit the prince to harm him physically or take any legal action against him. At worst, he would lose his best customers and suffer a tremendous loss of profit. This he willingly accepted for the sake of Shabbos.

The man's sons, boys in their teens, asked why he did not permit the gentile to take the key to his store and help himself to whatever he needed. Surely this would involve a smaller loss than that which he would probably suffer by refusing the prince's request. Hearing this, the man's aged father told his grandchildren, "Silence, children! Instead of offering your suggestions, you should rejoice over this great opportunity to make a sacrifice for the sake of God and His Torah. Listen to your father, and do not worry over the consequences."

After Shabbos, the man was summoned to Prince Hendrick's chambers. Fearing the worst, the man honored the summons and came before the prince. The prince welcomed him warmly and asked him to be seated. The prince said, "This past week, I had an argument with a friend. I maintained that a sincerely religious Jew places his beliefs above all. My friend, however, insisted that to the Jews, money comes before anything. We decided to test one Jew and see who was right. You were the one whom we chose. Obviously, you have passed the test and have proven me right."

From then on, the Jew was granted special privileges in doing business with the royal family. And when a member of the royal family visited the Land of Israel, he brought back a gift for the Jew — a pair of *tefillin* (from *Sefer L'Ch'vod Shabbos*).

While War Raged

◆§ Proper observance of Shabbos was a frequent theme of the Chofetz Chaim's writings and public addresses. In at least one instance, the Chofetz Chaim literally risked his life for the sake of Shabbos.

It was during World War I, in the summer of 1915. The German armies were advancing toward the Chofetz Chaim's town of Radin, and were almost certain to overrun the town. Using a system of lots that incorporates verses from the Torah and was revealed by the *Gaon of Vilna*, the Chofetz Chaim decided to leave Radin. Together with his family and those of a few very close disciples — including Rabbi Elchonon Wasserman — he headed for the Russian border.

Late Friday afternoon, the group found itself traveling by train near the town of Molodechno. The Chofetz Chaim turned to some family members and informed them that he would disembark from the train at its next stop, so as not to travel on Shabbos. He would spend Shabbos in the open fields, which was especially dangerous during wartime. The Chofetz Chaim is reported to have said, "You should continue on your journey. Without a doubt, traveling on Shabbos at such a time is surely permissible. As for me, I am prepared to risk my life for the sake of the Shabbos.[1]"

Immediately, Reb Elchonon announced that he and his family would remain in the fields with the Chofetz Chaim. The other disciples quickly followed suit. As they settled down in a field near a railroad crossing, danger was quickly apparent. The sentry at the crossing accused them of planning to sabotage the railroad tracks

---

1. R' Yosef Karo (*Yoreh Deah* 157:1) rules that it is permissible for one to give his life for the sake of a *mitzvah* at a time when he is not required to do so. This is at variance with the opinion of *Rambam* (*Hilchos Yesodei HaTorah* 5:4). However, with regard to *Rambam*'s ruling, *Nemukei Yosef* (*Sanhedrin* 74a) writes: ". . .Nevertheless, if one is a great personage, exceedingly pious, and possesses awe of Heaven, and he sees that the generation is lax with regard to this [i.e., *mitzvah* observance], it is permissible for him to sanctify the Name and give his life even for a [relatively] minor *mitzvah* — so that the people will take note of this and learn to fear the name of God and to love Him with all their heart."

and threatened to shoot should anyone make what he considered to be a wrong move. Later, a contingent of soldiers passing by amused themselves by hurling flaming torches at the terrified men, women and children. The group implored the Chofetz Chaim to board the next train. The Chofetz Chaim reiterated that everyone could and should travel — with the exception of himself. He now reasoned that *chillul Hashem*, desecration of Hashem's Name, made it impossible for him to travel. For were it to become known that he had boarded a train on Shabbos, unlearned people would reason that all halachic restrictions were relaxed during wartime.

About 4:00 that morning, one of the party, R' Mordechai Roitbatt, jumped onto a passing train heading toward Molodechno. He immediately alerted the community there to the dangers threatening the Chofetz Chaim and his group. He and a community leader hired a few horse-drawn wagons, and, placing their own lives in danger, headed to the fields. Heaven ordained that they should lose their way. By the time they located the group, it was late Shabbos afternoon and the danger had apparently passed. The sentry, having observed the behavior of the Jews since the previous night, had become their friend and protector. When it had begun to rain, he had invited the women and children to take shelter in his hut.

The Chofetz Chaim conducted *Shalosh Seudos* in the field, and spoke on the relationship between Shabbos, Redemption, and the current war. After *Ma'ariv* and *Havdalah*, the group made its way to Molodechno, where the Chofetz Chaim addressed the community — on the subject of Shabbos.